D1405362

Using STEM to Investigate Issues in Alternative Energy

Author: Barbara R. Sandall, Ed.D

Consultants: Schrylet Cameron and Suzanne Myers

Editors and Proofreader: Mary Dieterich, Sarah M. Anderson, and Margaret Brown

COPYRIGHT © 2011 Mark Twain Media, Inc.

ISBN 978-1-58037-578-8

Printing No. CD-404141

Mark Twain Media, Inc., Publishers
Distributed by Carson-Dellosa Publishing LLC

Visit us at www.carsondellosa.com

Table of Contents

Introduction to *Using STEM to Investigate Issues in Alternative Energy* iv

    Introduction to the Series iii

    Science, Technology, and Society iv

    Technological Design Process iv

    Mathematical Problem Solving v

    Research in Alternative Energy Fields v

Chapter One: Energy Issues 1

Chapter Two: Oil Spill Cleanup 16

Chapter Three: Air-Powered Vehicles 31

Chapter Four: Air Power – Wind 41

Chapter Five: Solar Power 53

Chapter Six: Biomass 68

Chapter Seven: Hydrogen Fuel Cells 76

Chapter Eight: STEM Design Challenge 92

APPENDICES

    Science Inquiry Skills Assessment 101

    Science Process Skills 103

    National Science Education Standards (NSES) 104

    Principles and Standards for School Mathematics (NCTM) 109

    International Standards for Technological Literacy (ITEA) 111

    Assessment Answer Keys 115

    References 116

Introduction to *Using STEM to Investigate Issues in Alternative Energy*

Introduction to the Series

The *STEMs of Learning: Science, Technology, Engineering, and Mathematics* is an initiative designed to get students interested in these career fields. In 2009, the National Academy of Engineering (NAE) and the National Research Council (NRC) reported that there is a lack of focus on the science, technology, engineering, and mathematics (STEM) subjects in K–12 schools. This creates concerns about the competitiveness of the United States in the global market and the development of a workforce with the knowledge and skills needed to address technical and technological issues. The focus of many current STEM education programs is on mathematics and science and not on engineering and technology. This series was developed to encourage students to become a part of the solution and increase interest in the STEM areas. The series introduces students to the use of STEM skills to solve problems. It is our hope that through these investigations students will become interested in the STEM areas of study.

The *Using STEM to Investigate Series* provides fun and meaningful integrated activities that cultivate an interest in topics in the STEM fields of science, technology, engineering, and mathematics and encourage students to explore careers in these fields. The series introduces students to the following topics: Issues in Alternative Energy, Issues in Food Production, and Issues in Managing Waste using science, mathematics, engineering, and technological design as a means for problem solving and scientific inquiry. Students actively engage in solving real-world problems using scientific inquiry, content knowledge, and technological design. All of the activities are aligned with the National Science Education (NSE) Standards, the National Council of Teachers of Mathematics (NCTM) Standards, and the International Technology Education Association (ITEA) Standards for Technological Literacy. For correlations to state, national, and Canadian provincial standards, visit www.carsondellosa.com.

The series is written for classroom teachers, parents, families, and students. The books in this series can be used as a full unit of study or as individual lessons to supplement existing curriculum programs or textbooks. Activities are designed to be pedagogically sound, hands-on minds-on activities that support the national standards. Parents and students can use this series as an enhancement to what is done in the classroom or as a tutorial at home. The procedures and content background are clearly explained in the introduction and within the individual activities. Materials used are commonly found in classrooms and homes or can be ordered from science supply sources. By using science inquiry and integrated activities, students will solve real-world problems and be encouraged to explore careers in the alternative energy fields. Each unit in this book provides content background information in alternative energy topics; hands-on activities that demonstrate how science, technology, engineering, and mathematics can be applied to problems in this field; and assessments that check students' mastery of the written material and the interactive projects.

Introduction to *Using STEM to Investigate Issues in Alternative Energy* (cont.)

Science, Technology, and Society

Science, technology, and society are very closely related. Science and technology have impacted personal and community health, population growth, natural resources, and environmental quality. It is important for students to understand the interrelationship of science, technology, and society because these factors impact their daily lives all over the world. Science advances new technology, and using new technology increases scientific knowledge.

Science and technology are pursued for different reasons. Science inquiry is driven by the desire to understand the natural world. Technology is driven by the need to solve problems and meet human needs. Technology usually has more of a direct effect on society. For example, the creation of the telephone, computers, and the Internet have had a large impact on the way our society communicates. Science and technology have also impacted the diagnoses and treatment of diseases, which has increased the longevity of the human race. Science and technology have created more comfortable places for us to live in most areas of the world. However, science and technology have also had a negative impact on our environment. As a new technology that we need or want is developed, the impact on the environment must be closely examined.

The National Science Education Standards (NSES) unifying concepts and science process skills integrate the areas of science, technology, engineering, and mathematics (STEM). The unifying concepts include systems, order, and organization; evidence, models, and explanations; change, constancy, and measurement; evolution and equilibrium; and form and function. The processes of inquiry are skills used in all content areas and in our everyday lives to investigate and solve problems. These science process skills include the basic skills of classifying, observing, measuring, inferring, communicating, predicting, manipulating materials, replicating, using numbers, developing vocabulary, questioning, and using cues. The integrated science process skills include creating models, formulating a hypothesis, generalizing, identifying and controlling variables, defining operationally, recording and interpreting data, making decisions, and experimenting.

Technological Design Process

The NSES recommend that students have abilities and understandings of technological design and about science and technology. The NSES Science and Technology Content Standard E states that "the technological design process includes identifying a problem or design opportunity; proposing designs and possible solutions; implementing the solution; evaluating the solution and its consequences; and communicating the problem, processes, and solution." Creativity, imagination, and a good content background are necessary in working in science and engineering.

The International Technology Education Association (ITEA) Standards for Technological Literacy also suggest that students develop abilities for a technological world that include applying the design process to solve a problem, using and maintaining technological products, and assessing the impact of the products on the environment and society. Students should have an understanding of the attributes of design and engineering design and the role of troubleshooting, research and development, inven-

Introduction to *Using STEM to Investigate Issues in Alternative Energy* (cont.)

tions and innovations, and experimentation in problem solving. The design process includes identifying and collecting information about everyday problems that can be solved by technology. It also includes generating ideas and requirements for solving the problems.

Mathematical Problem Solving

The National Council of Teachers of Mathematics (NCTM) recommend that students develop abilities to use problem-solving skills, formulate problems, develop and apply a variety of strategies to solve problems, verify and interpret results, and generalize solutions and strategies to new problems. Students also need to be able to communicate with models, orally, in writing, and with pictures and graphs; reflect and clarify their own thinking; use the skills of reading, listening, and observing to interpret and evaluate ideas; and be able to make conjectures and convincing arguments. Students should be able to recognize and apply reasoning processes, make and evaluate arguments, validate their own thinking, and use the power of reasoning to solve problems. All of these skills are related to science and technology, as well as mathematics.

Research in Alternative Energy Fields

The Intergovernmental Panel on Climate Change (IPCC) was formed in 1988. This group reviews the scientific research on climate change and offers assessments of climate change and its effects on the world. According to this agency, the greenhouse gas emissions due to human activity have increased 70 percent from 1970–2004. In the 2007 IPCC report, the largest growth has come from energy supply, transportation, and industry. In addition, natural sources of greenhouse gases include volcanic activity, animal emission, the release of carbon dioxide from the oceans and plants through the carbon cycle, and the presence of water vapor in the atmosphere through the water cycle. Based on the data collected from all continents and oceans, it was found that many of the natural Earth systems have been impacted by climate change. Some of the effects found were shrinking and decreased numbers of glaciers; increasing ground instability in permafrost regions and rock avalanches in mountain regions; changes in Arctic and Antarctic ecosystems; changes in hydrological systems; changes in terrestrial biological systems, such as earlier greening of vegetation in the spring; and changes in marine biological systems, such as water temperature, salinity, oxygen levels, circulation, and changes in ice cover.

Introduction to *Using STEM to Investigate Issues in Alternative Energy* (cont.)

According to the reports from the United Nations Framework Convention on Climate Change (UNFCCC), scientists believe that global climate change is causing drought, flooding, increased numbers of hurricanes and forest fires, rising sea levels, damage to crops, and rises in malaria. Global warming is caused by a combination of factors, one of which is an excess of greenhouse gases, such as carbon dioxide, methane, and nitrous oxide. These gases come mainly from burning fossil fuels, agriculture, and waste dumps. As temperatures increase, the amount of water vapor in the air also increases. When these gases are in the air, the sun's energy, which usually radiates back into space, is trapped, making the earth warmer.

There are concerns about the increasing dependence on oil imports, the stability of major oil-producing nations, and the remaining proven oil reserves on Earth. In addition, energy sources that have a lesser impact on the environment and do not contribute to greenhouse gases or other pollution are being sought. So there is a need to develop alternative energy sources. Alternative energy sources currently being investigated are air and wind energy, solar power, hybrids (using a combination of energy sources), hydrogen, wave energy, and geothermal energy. This book will investigate some of these alternative sources of energy and provide a challenge to students to develop some of the technology needed to use alternative sources of energy.

This series was developed to encourage students to become a part of the solution to the problem of fueling our desire for energy consumption. The series introduces students to the use of science, technology, engineering, and mathematics (STEM) to solve problems. It is our hope that through these investigations students will become interested in the STEM areas of study. This book focuses on the problems of using alternative energy and developing new technologies to make them more affordable.

Chapter One: Energy Issues

Teacher Information

Topic: Issues With Alternative Energy

Standards:
NSES – Unifying Concepts and Processes
Systems, Order, and Organization
Form and Function

NSES – Content
NSES E: Science and Technology
NSES F: Personal and Social Perspectives
NSES G: Science as a Human Endeavor

NCTM:
Problem Solving
Communication
Reasoning

ITEA:
Nature of Technology
Technology and Society

Concepts:
Pros of every energy source
Cons of every energy source

Objectives:
Students will be able to…
- Examine their own beliefs and values related to different sources of energy.
- Debate the issues, respecting the rights of others to maintain different rights and values.
- Evaluate possible solutions to the energy crisis.
- Explain what renewable and nonrenewable energy sources are.

Activity: Issues in Alternative Energy (p. 4)

Materials:
Issue Discussion Sheets

TEACHER NOTE: The major purpose of this activity is to help students learn about the issues involved in examining alternative energy sources. Prior to starting, the teacher should discuss the rules for discussion (i.e., all students have the right to their own opinions, they will listen and respect each other's ideas, etc.) Divide the class into groups of four. Reproduce the number of sets of sheets needed for groups of four students. Each group should have a set of issue discussion sheets.

Chapter One: | Energy Issues

Student Information

Topic: Issues With Alternative Energy

Concepts:
Pros of every energy source
Cons of every energy source

Objectives:
Students will be able to…
- Examine their own beliefs and values related to different sources of energy.
- Debate the issues, respecting the rights of others to maintain different rights and values.
- Evaluate possible solutions to the energy crisis.
- Explain what renewable and nonrenewable energy sources are.

Content Background:

    Energy is the ability to do work. **Work** in the scientific sense is moving something through a distance. Energy can come in many forms: electrical; nuclear; chemical; heat; sound; light; solar; geothermal; biomass; fossil fuels; the energy of water—hydroelectric, currents, waves, and tides; wind energy; energy from compressed air; mechanical; potential; and so on. Energy can be transformed from one form to another.

    Fossil fuels are the most used of the energy sources, but they are running out and cannot be quickly replaced. **Fossil fuels** are formed from organic matter trapped beneath the earth's surface. Coal, oil, and natural gas are fossil fuels. Fossil fuels also give off carbon dioxide when they are burned, which contributes to acid rain and greenhouse gases that affect global warming.

    Acid rain occurs when rain mixes with sulfates and nitrates given off from burning fossil fuels to form sulfuric and nitric acid.

    Greenhouse gases are formed when fossil fuels are burned and carbon dioxide is given off. The carbon dioxide and other gases trap the heat from the sun around the earth, making the atmosphere warmer. This is one of the causes of global warming. Burning fossil fuels releases approximately 6.5 billion metric tons of carbon dioxide a year.

    Plants take in carbon dioxide and release oxygen, which helps clean the air and reduce the amount of carbon dioxide. However, so much carbon dioxide is released into the air and more trees are being cut down every year that the remaining plants cannot remove it all. Fossil fuels can also cause pollution from oil tankers crashing into coral reefs, offshore drilling accidents, and leaks from pipelines and storage facilities on land.

    We need to start looking at alternative energy sources and developing the technology to use renewable energy. **Renewable energy** is en-

Chapter One: Energy Issues

Student Information

ergy that cannot be depleted or used up. Renewable energy sources include the sun, wind, water, agricultural residue, firewood, and animal dung.

Energy derived from the sun is solar energy. Hydroelectric energy is produced from water. Biomass is produced from wood, animal dung, and biodegradable wastes that produce energy when they are burned or chemically changed. Geothermal energy is produced from energy from inside the earth. Wave, tidal, and ocean thermal energy are produced from the motion of water in the oceans.

These sources of renewable energy cause less pollution and can often be used locally, which reduces transportation problems and costs. There is a need to identify renewable energy sources, constraints and trade-offs of using the renewable energy, and what technology and infrastructures are needed to use these resources.

There are pros and cons to be considered before selecting any new energy source. One example is ethanol. Ethanol is a fuel made from corn. It can be blended with gasoline to make a fuel called E85. It is a renewable domestic resource.

However, ethanol and E85 burn at hotter temperatures, so vehicles need specialized systems to run on this fuel. Only a few flex fuel vehicles can burn these fuels. Other disadvantages include that E85 produces less energy than gasoline and is more expensive to produce because it has to be blended with gasoline. Ethanol production also competes with other uses of corn, which is mainly food production.

Many other factors have to be considered when selecting an alternative energy source. One factor is developing the infrastructure to support a new fuel source, i.e., fueling stations. The balance of trade with other countries also will be impacted. The balance of trade is the difference between imports and exports over a given period of time.

Looking at alternative energy sources will also impact jobs from the goods and services industries. Corporations such as petroleum companies and refineries, companies that make parts for the transportation that we have, gas stations, etc., will all have to retool or run the risk of closing down.

Another consideration is the environmental impact of the new technologies. This includes not only how it impacts the environment when used, but also how the production of the components of the new technology affect the environment. There are no easy answers to the fuel crisis, so you need to be able to know how to find information and weigh the pros and cons of the issues to make intelligent decisions about the future.

More information on alternative fuels can be found in the issue discussion sheets: Offshore Drilling, Import More Foreign Oil, Solar Energy, Air/Wind Power, Biomass, Geothermal, Hydropower/Ocean/Wave Energy, Energy for Transportation. This activity will introduce alternative energy sources and some of the pros and cons of each source.

3

Name: _____   Date: _____

Chapter One: Energy Issues

Student Activity

Activity: Issues in Alternative Energy

Materials:
>   Issue Discussion Sheets

Challenge Question: Which alternative energy source is the best?

Procedure:
1.   Divide the class into groups of four. Give each group a set of issue discussion sheets.

2.   One person in the group chooses an issue discussion sheet and reads it to the group. That person then chooses which solution they believe is the best and explains why to the group.

3.   The other members of the group then share whether they agree or disagree and why they agree or disagree with the reader's choice.

4.   Have students continue reading and discussing until all of the issues have been covered.

Name: _____   Date: _____

Chapter One: Energy Issues

Alternative Energy Issue Discussion Sheets

- -

Issue 1 – Offshore Drilling

Approximately 574 million acres of Outer Continental Shelf are off-limits to oil drilling. An estimated 18 billion barrels of oil are located under the Outer Continental Shelf. Eighteen billion barrels of oil can provide enough fuel for the country for about 2 1/2 years. Oil companies and some members of the community would like to drill in these areas to produce more oil and reduce our dependence on foreign oil.

Environmentalists are concerned about the environmental impact of this offshore drilling. In 1981, Congress imposed a moratorium on new drilling. Since 2001, there have been 69 offshore deaths, 1,349 injuries, and 858 fires and explosions in the Gulf of Mexico.

On April 20, 2010, an explosion and fire occurred on a deepwater oil well in the Gulf of Mexico. Initial reports suggested that 1,000 barrels (42,000 gallons) of oil a day leaked from the pipe at the site of the oil well on the sea floor in the Gulf of Mexico. Later reports suggested the oil came out at the rate of 35,000 to 65,000 gallons/day. An investigation indicated that the blowout preventer, a safety precaution to cap the well in an emergency, did not function properly and did not cap the well. Oil washed up on beaches from Texas to Florida. Millions of fish, birds, and other sea animals came into direct contact with the oil. Costs to cap the well and contain and clean up the oil spill may reach over $5 billion dollars and could take years.

Question:
The United States consumes an estimated one-fourth of the world's oil, so what should we do?

Should we:

a. Increase the amount of offshore drilling so we can reduce our dependence on foreign oil?
b. Find ways to conserve energy so we do not need to do more offshore drilling?
c. Increase the offshore drilling with more mandated safety precautions?
d. End offshore drilling completely, and invest in more alternative energy sources?
e. Do something else? Explain.

Name:_____   Date:_____

Chapter One: Energy Issues

Alternative Energy Issue Discussion Sheets

- -

Issue 2 – Import More Foreign Oil

According to the U.S. Energy Administration, the United States imports 8.68 million barrels of oil per day. This oil comes from the Persian Gulf, Canada, Mexico, Nigeria, and Saudi Arabia, among other nations. One issue in importing oil is the transportation of the oil from its source to the United States.

One way to transport oil is by pipeline. Oil is pumped through a pipe from one location to another. Pipelines can be above ground, as they often are in Alaska, or buried underground. Pipelines can be built under oceans, but the costs associated with this method of transportation are too high, so most oil is shipped in tankers. The main problem with pipelines are that they can and do rupture, which can lead to oil spills and violent explosions.

Oil tankers are ships that carry the oil over the ocean to different ports around the world and in the United States. In, 1998, the *Exxon Valdez* headed from Valdez, Alaska, to Los Angeles, California. It struck a coral reef in Prince William Sound, Alaska, and lost 11 million gallons of oil. It impacted 1,100 miles of coastline in Alaska. There are still areas that are contaminated with that oil today.

Question:
The United States consumes an estimated one-fourth of the world's oil, so what should we do?

Should we:

a. Increase the amount of imported oil so we can continue to use more petroleum products?
b. Use railroads to transport oil from Canada and Mexico?
c. Build a pipeline from Canada and Mexico to bring the oil to the United States?
d. Build more fuel-efficient cars and reduce our use of petroleum products so it reduces the need for imports?
e. Do something else? Explain.

Name: _____ Date: _____

Chapter One: Energy Issues

Alternative Energy Issue Discussion Sheets

- -

Issue 3: Solar Energy

Solar energy is produced from the energy from the sun. It can be used to heat, cool, and light our homes and businesses. Solar water heating, passive solar systems used to heat and cool buildings, and photovoltaic cells that convert sunlight directly into electricity are the most common technologies for using solar energy at this time. Some of these technologies are expensive to install but will save money on heating and cooling bills in the long run.

Solar energy has also been used to power cars. The GM SunRaycer was a prototype car fueled by an array of solar voltaic cells. The technology used to power the SunRaycer led to the development of electric vehicles. The 2010 Toyota Prius uses solar power to run a fan that cools the car's interior, which reduces the amount of gasoline needed to power the air conditioner.

The advantages of solar energy are it is a clean fuel and it is a renewable resource. The disadvantage is that the sun does not always shine, so there needs to be a way to store the energy for later use. The initial cost of the equipment to capture and convert solar energy to electricity is also expensive.

Question: How can we encourage more people and businesses to use solar power?

Should we:

a. Put solar panels on every home to heat and cool the houses, making the homeowners pay for the panels?
b. Install solar arrays on the rooftops of all large buildings in the cities to heat and cool tall buildings and provide electrical power to the buildings?
c. Have the government give rebates to everyone who adds solar power to their houses?
d. Sell the excess electricity produced by solar panels on homes to the utility companies or place it in storage for use when extra power is needed?
e. Do something else? Explain.

Name: _____   Date: _____

Chapter One: Energy Issues

Alternative Energy Issue Discussion Sheets

- -

Issue 4: Air/Wind Power

The advantage of using wind power is that it is a renewable resource that does not pollute the earth. In areas where wind is fairly constant, wind power is an economical and clean power source. Wind farms can be located on land or offshore in the water. Since wind turbines take up little space on the ground, farmers can lease land to utility companies for wind turbines while still being able to farm most of the land.

One disadvantage with this renewable source of energy is that it only works when the wind is blowing. Other problems with the wind turbines are birds and bats occasionally fly into them. Turbines generate a constant noise as they turn. Some people find the shadow flicker from the motion of the blades annoying. Some people don't like how the wind turbines look or the sounds they make.

In most places, there are regulations about how far away from existing houses, businesses, and other structures a wind turbine can be built. This helps lessen the impact of the noise, shadow flicker, and unsightliness on nearby residents.

Question: How can we increase the percentage of our energy produced by wind turbines without negatively impacting the environment and the people who live nearby?

Should we:

a. Develop more wind farms all over the world? It does not matter if birds fly into them.
b. Develop wind turbines that have less impact on the natural environment so they do not harm birds?
c. Use wind turbines in conjunction with solar panels, so that when the wind is not blowing, there is another source of energy?
d. Strategically place the wind turbines in the middle of nowhere were people will not see them?
e. Do something else? Explain.

Name: _____ Date: _____

Chapter One: Energy Issues

Alternative Energy Issue Discussion Sheets

- -

Issue 5: Biomass

Biomass energy comes from plants and plant-derived materials. Examples of biomass are wood, food crops (such as corn and soybeans), grassy and woody plants, residues from agriculture and forestry (such as husks, stalks, and sawdust), oil-rich algae, and the organic components of municipal and industrial wastes. Methane, a natural gas from landfills, is also a product of biomass.

One advantage of using biomass is it can reduce greenhouse gases by balancing the carbon dioxide in the atmosphere. Biomass only releases as much or less carbon dioxide as the plants used during growth. Another advantage of biomass fuels is that it can reduce our dependence on foreign oil. Biomass supports the U.S. forestry and agricultural industries. Because so many types of plant material can be converted to biomass fuels, people around the world can use what is available and cheap.

Disadvantages of using biomass to produce energy include losing forests and cropland to the production of biomass. The cost of food could go up if too much land is used for growing biomass instead of food crops. Also, burning biomass does release carbon dioxide into the atmosphere. It can also be too expensive to produce biomass fuels.

E85 fuel, gasoline with 85 percent ethanol, is one example of using biomass energy. Another is using used cooking grease to power cars equipped with biodesiel engines.

Question: How can we encourage more research in the use of biomass for fuel?

Should we:

a. Have the government mandate research and development of the use of biomass to cut back on the consumption of nonrenewable energy?
b. Have the government fund research that would develop new technologies to use biofuels?
c. Have companies offer rewards for inventors who can come up with ways of efficiently and inexpensively processing biomass into biofuels?
d. Only drive cars that will use E85 or other biofuels?
e. Do something else? Explain

Name: _____   Date: _____

Chapter One: Energy Issues

Alternative Energy Issue Discussion Sheets

‒ ‒

Issue 6: Geothermal

Geothermal energy is produced as a result of the hot magma beneath the earth's surface. Geothermal power plants use pumps to pull up the heat energy from below the surface of the earth. The heat energy is then either used to produce electricity by creating steam from water, or it is pumped directly into homes for heating. Hot springs, where the heat from within the earth heats surface water, are the most visible source of geothermal power. The heat is most accessible along tectonic plate lines.

Geothermal energy can be used to heat and cool homes or businesses. Heat pumps are one way of tapping into geothermal energy. Underground homes also use geothermal energy for heating and cooling. In the western United States, many people get clean energy from geothermal power plants.

The advantages of geothermal energy are that it is renewable and it requires no other fuel to produce heat or electricity. Geothermal power plants use less land per megawatt than other types of power plants.

However, there are disadvantages to geothermal energy. Drilling for and building a geothermal power plant is expensive. Likewise, the initial installation costs for a geothermal heat pump are higher than conventional heating and cooling systems. Regular geothermal power plants can usually only be built near the edge of tectonic plates. Drilling for enhanced geothermal power plants, located away from tectonic plate lines, has triggered thousands of earthquakes. Geothermal fluids can release carbon dioxide and hydrogen sulfide and can contain mercury, arsenic, and antimony. These substances can pollute the air and water, contribute to global warming, and produce a bad smell.

Question: How can we take greater advantage of geothermal energy stored in the earth?

Should we:

a. Convert all homes and businesses to geothermal energy for heating and cooling?
b. Ask the state and federal government to give tax incentives or rebates to people who put in geothermal heating and cooling systems?
c. Build more geothermal power plants along the edges of tectonic plates?
d. Drill for enhanced geothermal power plants in areas away from tectonic plate edges?
e. Do something else? Explain.

Name: _____ Date: _____

Chapter One: Energy Issues

Alternative Energy Issue Discussion Sheets

- -

Issue 7: Hydropower/Ocean/Wave Energy

Hydropower or waterpower is power made by using the movement of water to power machines or make electricity. The water is not used up, because the water cycle continuously renews the water. Hydroelectric power is produced when moving water turns a turbine that is connected to a generator that makes electricity. The most common form of hydropower is constructing dams that control the flow of a river and use the moving water to turn turbines to create electricity.

Scientists are now building devices that will capture the energy from tides and ocean currents to produce electricity. They are also using ocean thermal energy conversion (using the heat in ocean water) to produce electricity. The use of ocean waves, currents, and tides are just now being investigated, so we have little data on the impact of these devices on the environment. These new technologies are also very expensive.

The advantages of hydropower are it is a clean source of energy, and it is a domestic source of energy. Building dams to control the flow of rivers to produce electricity also creates reservoirs for recreation, fishing, swimming, and boating. Dams can help control flooding. They are also a predictable and dependable source of energy.

The disadvantage of using hydroelectric dams is the impact on the environment. The change in the flow of the river may change habitats up and downstream. Some existing river areas may be flooded while some may lose their water supply because of the reduced flow. Dams can also fail, causing flooding, property damage, and loss of life.

Question: How can we better use hydroelectric, ocean, and wave energy to produce electricity?

Should we:

a. Set up dams on all rivers to create hydroelectric power plants for all river communities?
b. Set up wave and current generators because we need the power?
c. Set up more dams and ocean generators because it will produce more jobs?
d. Invest in more research to find out what the environmental impacts of wave, current, and tidal devices are?
e. Do something else? Explain

Name: _____   Date: _____

Chapter One: Energy Issues

Alternative Energy Issue Discussion Sheets

- -

Issue 8: Energy for Transportation

One of the largest uses for energy is in transportation. The higher our transportation costs, the higher our goods and services cost. Transportation also contributes to greenhouse gases, one of our major sources of pollution.

Solar energy has been used to power cars. The GM SunRaycer was a prototype car fueled by an array of solar voltaic cells. While solar vehicles are not commercially viable, the technology used in the SunRaycer led directly to electric vehicles.

Electric cars were invented in 1830. In 1996, GM built the first commercially available electric car, the EV-1. The car required no fuel and could be plugged in at home to charge it. The Chevrolet Volt is the most promising of the next generation of electric/hybrid cars.

Honda, Toyota, and Ford have developed technology for hybrid cars. The hybrids run on gas or electricity depending on how much energy is needed. Hybrid cars currently reach 30–58 mpg. Most of the high-mileage cars are smaller cars.

Compressed air can power a small car or van. It can reach 70 mph and can run 125 miles on a tank of air on flat roads. Compressed air was used in locomotives and trams in the late 1800s, but pressure from oil companies blocked commercial use.

Biomass is made of organic plant materials. It is a renewable energy source. Biomass can be burned or converted chemically into fuel. Corn and soy oils can be used to fuel cars and trucks.

Hydrogen is an element found in many different compounds. The only by-product from using hydrogen is water. Vehicles with fuel cells combine hydrogen and water to produce electricity and heat. Hydrogen is highly reactive and does not occur naturally. Other energy sources must be used to create it, and then it can be stored for later use. Three issues in the use of hydrogen are improving the fuel cell technology, producing the hydrogen efficiently and cost-effectively, and building the infrastructure to support hydrogen filling stations.

Question: How can we reduce our oil consumption, reduce pollution, conserve energy, and start using some of these energy alternatives in transportation?

Should:
a. The government tax cars that do not get good mileage?
b. The government force automobile makers to produce cars that get a minimum of 30 miles/gallon?
c. Everyone carpool, take public transportation, ride bikes, or walk to cut back on driving?
d. Everyone only buy fuel-efficient non-polluting cars so that car manufacturers will only build these kinds of vehicles?
e. Car manufactures build cars that use alternative fuels to reduce pollution and oil consumption?
f. We do something else? Explain.

Chapter One: Energy Issues

Investigate Further: Alternative Energy Sources

Websites

Chicago Museum of Science and Industry: Smart Home

http://www.msichicago.org/whats-here/exhibits/smart-home/

Future Cars: Human Car

http://www.futurecars.com/future-cars/electric-cars/earth-day-special-the-human-car-hc-imagineps

Horizon Fuel Cell Technology Kits

http://www.horizonfuelcell.com/

National Energy Education Development (NEED) Project

http://www.need.org/

NEED Elementary Energy Infobook

http://www.need.org/needpdf/ElementaryEnergyInfobook.pdf

NEED Global Climate Change

http://www.need.org/needpdf/infobook_activities/SecInfo/Global.pdf

NEED History of Energy

http://www.need.org/needpdf/infobook_activities/ElemInfo/HistoryE.pdf

NEED Intermediate Energy InfoBook

http://www.need.org/needpdf/IntermediateEnergyInfobook.pdf

NEED Intro to Energy

http://www.need.org/needpdf/infobook_activities/IntInfo/Introl.pdf

NEED Saving Energy Student/Family Guide

http://www.need.org/needpdf/SavingEnergyStudent Guide.pdf

NEED Secondary Energy InfoBook

http://www.need.org/needpdf/SecondaryEnergyInfobook.pdf

National Renewable Energy Laboratory

http://www.nrel.gov/learning/re_basics.html

NOVA: Car of the Future

http://www.pbs.org/wgbh/nova/car/open/

Think Global Green

http://www.thinkglobalgreen.org

Think Global Green: Conservation

http://www.thinkglobalgreen.org/CONSERVATION.html

Think Global Green: Geothermal Energy

http://www.thinkglobalgreen.org/GEOTHERMAL.html

Think Global Green: Electric Vehicles

http://www.thinkglobalgreen.org/ELECTRICVEHICLES.html

Think Global Green: Natural Gas

http://www.thinkglobalgreen.org/NATURALGAS.html

Think Global Green: Nuclear Power

http://www.thinkglobalgreen.org/NUCLEAR.html

Think Global Green: Off-Shore Drilling

http://www.thinkglobalgreen.org/OFFSHOREDRILLING.html

Think Global Green: Solar Power

http://www.thinkglobalgreen.org/SOLAR.html

Think Global Green: Wave Power

http://www.thinkglobalgreen.org/WAVEPOWER.html

Think Global Green: Wind Power

http://www.thinkglobalgreen.org/WINDPOWER.html

U.S. Energy Information Administration: Energy Kids

http://tonto.eia.doe.gov/kids/energy.cfm?page=2

Hydrogen

http://tonto.eia.doe.gov/kids/energy.cfm?page=hydrogen_home-basics

Video Resources

Who Killed the Electric Car? DVD

http://www.whokilledtheelectriccar.com/

Name: _____ Date: _____

Chapter One: Energy Issues

Alternative Energy Assessment

Objectives:

Students will be able to:

- Examine their own beliefs and values related to different sources of energy.
- Debate the issues, respecting the rights of others to maintain different rights and values.
- Evaluate possible solutions to the energy crisis.

Matching: Match the type of alternative energy with its definition.

_____ 1. Solar Energy

a. Energy, captured from the uneven heating and cooling of the atmosphere, drives a turbine, which converts the energy of the moving air into electrical energy

_____ 2. Geothermal Energy

b. Energy from the sun that can be used directly for heating, cooling, generating electricity, heating water, etc.

_____ 3. Wind Energy

c. Uses hydrogen to generate electricity to power vehicles

_____ 4. Compressed Air Energy

d. Energy from the hot magma inside of the earth used for generating electricity and heating and cooling buildings

_____ 5. Hydroelectric Power

e. Energy produced by moving water turning a generator to produce electricity

_____ 6. Hydrogen Fuel Cells

f. Energy produced from ocean tides as a result of the gravitational pull of the moon and sun on the earth; also energy captured from the motion of waves, currents, and the heat in the ocean water

_____ 7. Biomass Energy

g. Energy from air that has been under pressure that can be used to power vehicles

_____ 8. Ocean / Wave Energy

h. Use of organic matter—plants and animal matter—to produce electricity, transportation fuels, or chemicals

Name: _____ Date: _____

9. Explain some of the advantages and disadvantages of each of the fuels on the previous page.

_____

_____

_____

_____

_____

_____

_____

_____

_____

_____

_____

_____

_____

_____

10. If you had to decide which energy sources to use, which would you pick? Why?

_____

_____

_____

_____

11. Which is the most important consideration when evaluating energy sources to use: economic issues, impact on the environment, political issues, or other considerations?

_____

_____

_____

12. Explain the difference between a renewable energy source and a nonrenewable energy source.

_____

_____

_____

_____

Chapter Two: Oil Spill Cleanup

Teacher Information

Topic: Oil Spill Cleanup

Standards:
NSES – Unifying Concepts and Processes
Systems, Order, and Organization
Form and Function

NSES – Content
NSES A: Science as Inquiry
NSES B: Physical Science
NSES C: Life Science
NSES D: Earth Science
NSES E: Science and Technology
NSES G: Science as a Human Endeavor

NCTM:
Problem Solving
Communication
Statistics – Data collection and analysis
Numbers
Number Systems
Computation

ITEA:
Nature of Technology
Technology and Society
Understanding and Abilities in Engineering
Design

Concepts:
Difficulty of cleaning up an oil spill
How oil and water react
Environmental impact of oil spills
Constraints
Trade-offs

Objectives:
Students will be able to…
• Identify some of the problems with cleaning up an oil spill.

• Describe some of the constraints and trade-offs that need to be made to clean up an oil spill.
• Describe what happens to the wildlife and habitats around an oil spill.
• Identify the advantages and disadvantages of fossil fuels.
• Identify a problem; create a solution for the problem; construct, test, evaluate, and redesign the model as needed; design the cleanup; identify the constraints and trade-offs made in cleaning up an oil spill; and communicate the results.

Activity: Cleaning Up an Oil Spill (p. 20)

Materials: (for each group)
    stop watch   food coloring
    clear plastic container (the size of a
        shoebox)
    water (enough to fill the container
        halfway)
    vegetable oil
    clay   cheesecloth
    filter paper or coffee filters
    plastic overhead sheets or clear report
        covers
    funnels   sponges
    straws   cotton balls
    other containers   yarn
    nylon stockings
    other materials students think might be
        used in oil cleanup
    writing paper   pencils
    poster paper   calculators

Chapter Two: Oil Spill Cleanup

Student Information

Topic: Oil Spill Cleanup

Concepts:
Difficulty of cleaning up an oil spill
How oil and water react
Environmental impact of oil spills
Constraints
Trade-offs

Objectives:
Students will be able to…
- Identify some of the problems with cleaning up an oil spill.
- Describe some of the constraints and trade-offs that need to be made to clean up an oil spill.
- Describe what happens to the wildlife and habitats around an oil spill.
- Identify the advantages and disadvantages of fossil fuels.
- Identify a problem; create a solution for the problem; construct, test, evaluate, and redesign the model as needed; design the cleanup; identify the constraints and trade-offs made in cleaning up an oil spill; and communicate the results.

Content Background:

In the areas surrounding the United States' coastlines, known as the Outer Continental Shelf, there are about 574 million acres of land under ocean waters that contain an estimated 18 billion barrels of oil. These 18 billion barrels of oil alone can fuel the country for two and a half years.

Oil companies and some members of the community would like to drill in these areas to produce more oil and reduce our dependence on foreign oil. Environmentalists are concerned about the environmental impact of this offshore drilling. In 1981, Congress imposed a moratorium on new drilling.

Since 2001, there have been 69 offshore deaths, 1,349 injuries, and 858 fires and explosions in the Gulf of Mexico. On April 20, 2010, an explosion and fire occurred on a British Petroleum (BP) deepwater oil rig in the Gulf of Mexico. Initial reports suggested that 1,000 barrels (42,000 gallons) of oil a day leaked from the oil well on the sea floor in the Gulf of Mexico. Later reports suggested the oil came out at the rate of 35,000 to 65,000 gallons a day. An investigation indicated that the blowout preventer, a safety precaution to cap the well in an emergency, did not function properly, so it did not cap the well.

Throughout the summer of 2010, BP struggled to find a way to cap the well, located a mile from the ocean surface. Finally on July 15, the well was successfully capped. It was permanently killed by pumping cement into a relief well drilled through the sea bed and was declared "effectively dead" on September 19. The cleanup of this oil spill will cost billions of dollars, and some areas of marshlands, beaches, and aquatic habitats may never be cleaned up completely. The devastation to maritime animals is almost too great to calculate. People who depend on the sea for their business, such as fishermen, shrimpers, restaurant owners, and others in the tourism industry, lost millions of dollars in income during and after the spill. BP is being held responsible for the cleanup and is compensating those who suffered losses.

Chapter Two: Oil Spill Cleanup

Student Information

Another source of oil in the United States other than from offshore drilling is imported oil. This oil is shipped by tanker ships, piped from the Alaskan pipeline, or moved by other forms of transportation. According to the U.S. Energy Administration, the United States imports 8.68 million barrels of oil per day. The oil imports come from the Persian Gulf, Canada, Mexico, Nigeria, and Saudi Arabia, among other countries.

One issue in importing oil is the volatility of the governments in some of the largest oil-producing countries.

Another issue involved in importing oil is the transportation of the oil from its source to the United States. Pipelines transport oil over land. Oil tankers carry the oil over the ocean to different ports around the world and in the United States.

In 1989, the tanker *Exxon Valdez* headed from Valdez, Alaska, to Los Angeles, California, struck a coral reef in Prince William Sound, Alaska, and lost 11 million gallons of oil. It impacted 1,100 miles of coastline in Alaska. The oil stuck to the feathers of ducks, geese, and other seabirds, and they could not swim or fly. Over 300,000 birds died. The oil also got into the bodies of fish, shrimp, crabs, sea otters, seal lions, seals, and whales, and thousands of them died. In 2010, there are still areas that are contaminated with this oil.

The cleanup of oil spills of this magnitude is difficult. The oil spreads out and floats on top of the water because oil and water do not mix. Cleanup crews must try to contain the spill and then try to collect the oil using skimmers and special absorbent pads.

In larger spills, they may try to burn off the oil or use chemicals to disperse the oil, but these actions have negative side effects. Burning sends smoke and gas in the air and ash in the water. Chemicals break the oils apart or make the oil come together so it can be picked up, but the chemicals can also add poisons to the water.

When the oil comes to shore, workers may use power washers to push the oil out to sea. However, it sometimes just pushes the oil further into the rocks and sand, which can harm plants and animals. Scientists may add bacteria to eat the oil, but large spills would require a lot of bacteria.

Sometimes the scientists decide that doing nothing is the best way to clean it up. In that case, the winds and waves make the oil mix with the water, and it eventually breaks down. There is no easy way to clean up an oil spill. There are always trade-offs that have to be made.

One way to prevent oil spills is using less oil with more fuel-efficient cars, driving less, and driving the speed limit. Other ways of limiting the impact of oils spills are constructing the oil tankers out of better materials, teaching people how to contain and clean up oil spills more quickly, and developing new and better ways to clean up the slick.

Oil spills affect the wildlife and habitats in the area of the spill. The U.S. Fish and Wildlife Service is a federal agency that oversees fish and wildlife resources and habitats. The Fish and Wildlife Service reports that there were 33 National Wildlife Refuges at risk from the British Petroleum *Deepwater Horizon* oil spill in 2010. The wildlife refuges affected are along the coast of Louisiana, Mississippi, Alabama, and Florida. These refuges are homes to threatened and endangered species.

Chapter Two: Oil Spill Cleanup

Student Information

The impact on wildlife and habitats depends on the type and quantity of oil spilled, as well as the season, weather, type of shoreline, and the tides in the area of the spill. Types of oil are classified by the density, such as crude, light crude, etc. Most oil is less dense than water, so it floats on water. The oil spreads on the surface of the water.

When the oil undergoes weathering, it introduces more toxic materials into the water. **Weathering** is the physical, chemical, and biological changes that occur when oil interacts with the environment. This weathering is caused by oil being exposed to air, sunlight, waves, tides, and microscopic organisms. How fast it weathers is determined by the type of oil, the shoreline, and the ocean floor in the area of the spill.

When animals come into contact with oil, they can be harmed when they ingest the oil (either by eating it directly or eating contaminated fish or plants), absorb the oil through their skin, or inhale oil particles.

The oil contaminates the plankton that fish and other wildlife eat, and then they become contaminated. **Plankton** includes algae, fish eggs, and larvae. Larger organisms in the food chain, including humans, eat the contaminated fish and become contaminated.

Birds that have been covered in oil lose their ability to fly, dive for food, or float on the water, which can lead to drowning. Bird feathers naturally repel water, but oil interferes with this and can cause hypothermia, leading the birds to freeze to death. Birds can ingest (swallow) the oil when they are preening (cleaning) their feathers. Swallowing oil can kill them instantly or may damage the lungs, liver, and kidneys.

Sea turtles also may swallow the oil. Their nesting areas on shore may be destroyed, as well as the eggs that have been laid. Shellfish that live in the bottom of the oceans may also be contaminated.

Fish and shellfish can become contaminated through their gills, by ingesting the oil, and by eating food covered with oil. Shellfish include lobsters, crabs, clams, oysters, and others. The oil may contaminate their habitats and decrease the probability of the survival of their eggs. Contaminated fish may have stunted growth, enlarged livers, changes in their heart and respiration rates, deteriorated fins, and damage to their reproductive systems.

Scavengers in the food chain eat the carcasses of the contaminated dead animals and become contaminated themselves.

Plants can also be impacted by oil spills. Seaweed may be killed. Algae may die or become more abundant after an oil spill, depending on the species of algae.

The oil spilled tends to stay in the environment long after the spill occurs, so it has a long-term impact on the habitats of the area. Oil has been found in ocean sediment 30 years after a spill.

There are many problems with depending on petroleum as our major source of energy. In the following investigations, you will investigate some of the problems with the transportation of and offshore drilling of crude oil. You will also investigate the problems of cleaning up after a spill.

Name: _____   Date: _____

Chapter Two: Oil Spill Cleanup
Student Activity

Activity: Cleaning Up an Oil Spill

Challenge Question: What is the best way to clean up an oil spill?

Adapted from BSCS TRACS Designing Environmental Solutions and NSTA Picture Perfect Science

Materials:

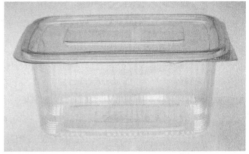

Food coloring
Clear plastic container (the size of a shoebox)
Water (enough to fill the container halfway)
1 Tbsp vegetable oil
Clay
Cheesecloth
Filter paper or coffee filters
Funnels
Plastic overhead sheets or clear report covers
Sponges
Straws
Cotton balls
Other containers
Nylon stockings
Yarn
Dish soap
Other materials
Writing paper

Procedure:

Part 1 – Create an Oil Spill
1. Cover your area with newspaper
2. Place a few drops of food coloring in the water in the clear container.
3. Pour 1 Tbsp vegetable oil into the water.

Brainstorm:
1. Examine the materials provided.
2. Brainstorm how you might use the materials to clean up the oil spill you created.
3. Record all of the suggestions team members recommend.
4. Go through all of the ideas and narrow the list down to three or four ideas to clean up the spill.

Name: _____   Date: _____

Chapter Two: Oil Spill Cleanup

Student Activity

Part Two – Materials for Cleanup

1. Examine the materials provided and discuss with your group what you might use to clean up the spill.

Cheesecloth	Filter paper or coffee filters	Funnels
Plastic overhead sheets or clear report covers		Sponges
Straws	Cotton balls	Nylon stockings
Yarn	Dish soap	Other containers
Other materials		

2. Make a list of the materials above that the team wants to test.

    _____

    _____

    _____

    _____

3. Get a small amount of each material to test.
4. Decide how to test the materials and record the procedure you will use to test each material.

    _____

    _____

    _____

    _____

    _____

    _____

    _____

    _____

Name: _____ Date: _____

Chapter Two: Oil Spill Cleanup

Student Activity

5. Test your materials
6. Record your results in the data table below.

Material	Observations

7. Which materials worked best? Why?

_____

_____

_____

_____

_____

_____

Name: _____   Date: _____

Chapter Two: Oil Spill Cleanup

Student Activity

Part Three – Designing the Cleanup Plan

Materials:

       Pencil   Paper   Poster paper   Calculators

Three things must be considered when you are developing an oil spill cleanup plan—the cost, time, and completeness.

1. Plan a way to clean up the oil spill inexpensively, quickly, or thoroughly.

   Cost: The plan must help your team clean up the spilled oil inexpensively.

   Time: The plan must help your team clean up the spilled oil quickly.

   Completeness: The plan must help your team clean up the spilled oil thoroughly.

2. Use the following chart to determine the cost of your cleanup solution.

Item	Cost
Clay	65 cents each
Cheesecloth	25 cents each
Filter Paper	10 cents / circle
Funnels	80 cents each
Plastic Sheets	20 cents each
Sponges	35 cents each
Straws	5 cents each
Cotton Balls	5 cents each
Other containers	0 recycled
Yarn	5 cents a meter
Nylon Stockings	0 recycled
Dish Soap	12 cents an ounce

3. Discuss your ideas in your team. Discuss the positive and negative consequences of using each plan.
4. Decide which of the three things to consider you think is the most important.

Name: _____   Date: _____

Chapter Two: Oil Spill Cleanup

Student Activity

5.   Design a plan to solve the problem you have selected. Use the space below for your notes. Write out your finished plan on your own paper.
   a.   Record your operational definitions of what you mean by inexpensively, quickly, and thoroughly.
   b.   Identify all of the details of the plan.
   c.   List all of the costs involved in the plan.
   d.   Record exactly what you will do.
   e.   Describe how you will know the plan was successful.
   f.   Create a data table to record your data.

_____

_____

_____

_____

_____

_____

_____

_____

_____

_____

_____

_____

_____

_____

_____

_____

_____

_____

_____

_____

_____

Name: _____ Date: _____

Chapter Two: Oil Spill Cleanup

Student Activity

Part Four – Test Your Plan

Materials:

Stop watch	Food coloring
Clear plastic container (the size of a shoebox)	
Water (enough to fill the container halfway)	
1 Tbsp vegetable oil	
Clay	Cheesecloth
Filter paper or coffee filters	Funnels
Plastic overhead sheets or clear report covers	
Sponges	Straws
Cotton balls	Other containers
Nylon stockings	Yarn
Dish soap	Other materials
Paper	Poster paper

1. Create an oil spill like you did in Part One.
2. Start the stop watch as soon as you put in the oil.
3. Follow the team plan that you made in Part Three exactly.
4. On your own paper, record what you did.
5. Record how long it took.
6. Record how much money the team spent on materials for the cleanup.
7. Record how the team will decide how thorough the cleanup is.
8. Record how effective your cleanup was.
9. On poster paper, record how much the plan costs, how quickly the plan works, or how much oil the team's plan removes. Share your plan and your results with the rest of the class.

Discussion:

1. Which team had the most inexpensive plan? _____

2. Which team had the quickest plan? _____

3. Which team had the most thorough plan? _____

4. Which team's plan was the most successful if you needed a plan that was inexpensive, quick, and

    thorough? _____

Name: _____   Date: _____

Chapter Two: Oil Spill Cleanup

Student Activity

Part Five – Constraints and Trade-offs

When developing any new technologies and deciding what will work best, there are always constraints and trade-offs. Constraints are things that limit what can be done. In the oil spill investigation, the constraints included the amount and kind of oil, the amount of water, the area covered, and materials available to use for the cleanup. Another constraint might be the physical behavior of the oil in the water. Oil will not mix with water, and it is less dense than water, so it floats. These are all things that you have no control over during the cleanup investigation.

In solving the oil spill cleanup problem, there are also trade-offs. In designing the solution, the consequences of what you do to clean up the spill are considered because the solution may have negative consequences. Other considerations are if it was more important to save money or save time. What you do to clean up the spill may cause more damage than the oil would. The solution you choose may depend on your values, personal preferences, how you determine what is "clean enough", and how much money you are willing to spend. Your point of view may also be influenced by how close you are to the spill, whether you work for the oil company or a conservation group, etc. In the investigations in Parts Three and Four, you had to decide what trade-offs you were willing to make to get the oil spill cleaned up. You had to choose between the cost, time, and thoroughness of the cleanup.

Discussion:

1. In real oil spills, what would be some constraints to consider before you started to clean up the spill?

    _____

    _____

    _____

    _____

    _____

    _____

2. In real oil spills, what trade-offs would you be willing to make?

    _____

    _____

    _____

    _____

    _____

    _____

Name: _____   Date: _____

Chapter Two: Oil Spill Cleanup

Student Activity

3. Explain what you think will happen if sea birds are covered with crude oil.

    _____

    _____

    _____

    _____

    _____

    _____

4. How does an oil spill impact other living things?

    _____

    _____

    _____

    _____

    _____

    _____

    _____

    _____

    _____

    _____

    _____

Challenge:

1. Devise a plan to clean up the oil along the Gulf Coast.

2. Devise a better off-shore drilling process that will protect our wildlife and the fishing industry.

Chapter Two: Oil Spill Cleanup

Investigate Further: Oil Drilling, Oil Spills, and Cleanup

British Petroleum
http://www.bp.com/extendedsectiongeneric
article.do?categoryID=40&contentID=7061813

Department of the Interior
http://www.doi.gov

The Encyclopedia of Earth: *Exxon Valdez* **Oil Spill**
http://www.eoearth.org/article/Exxon_Valdez_
oil_spill

Environmental Protection Agency
http://www.epa.gov/

Intergovernmental Panel on Climate Change
http://www.ipcc.ch/

International Bird Rescue Research Center
http://www.ibrrc.org/

Marine Mammal Center, Sausalito, CA
http://www.marinemammalcenter.org/

National Wildlife Rehabilitators Association
http://www.nwrawildlife.org/home.asp

NEED: Energy Consumption
http://www.need.org/needpdf/infobook_
activities/IntInfo/Consl.pdf

NEED: Petroleum
http://www.need.org/needpdf/infobook_
activities/IntInfo/Petrol.pdf

SeaWorld and Busch Gardens Conservation Fund
http://www.swbg-conservationfund.org/

Think Global Green: Off-Shore Drilling
http://www.thinkglobalgreen.org/OFFSHORE
DRILLING.html

Tri-State Bird Rescue and Research Newark, DE
http://www.tristatebird.org/

United States Coast Guard: Restore the Gulf
http://www.restorethegulf.gov/

U.S. Energy Information Administration
http://eia.doe.gov/

U.S. Fish and Wildlife Service
http://www.fws.gov/home/dhoilspill

Effects of Oil on Wildlife and Habitat
http://www.fws.gov/home/dhoilspill/pdfs/
DHJICFWSOilImpactsWildlifeFactSheet.pdf

Articles

BBC News (May 21, 2010) "US Coast Guard Sets Fire to Oil Leaking in the Gulf."
http://news.bbc.co.uk/2/hi/americas/8649862.
stm

Olvera, Jennifer. (2008) "5 Things You Need to Know About Oil Dependency"
http://www.greencar.com/articles/5-things-
need-oil-dependency.php

Olvera, Jennifer. (2008) "5 Things You Need to Know About Petroleum Violation Escrow Account"
http://www.greencar.com/articles/5-things-
need-petroleum-violation-escrow-account.php

Books

Rand, Gloria. (1994) *Prince William.* New York: Holt and Company.

Smith, Roland. (2003) *Sea Otter Rescue: The Aftermath of an Oil Spill.* New York: Puffin.

Name: _____   Date: _____

Chapter Two: Oil Spill Cleanup

Oil Spill Assessment

Objectives:
Students will be able to…
- Identify some of the problems with cleaning up an oil spill.
- Describe some of the constraints and trade-offs that need to be made to clean up an oil spill.
- Describe what happens to the wildlife and habitats around an oil spill.
- Identify a problem; create a solution for the problem; construct, test, evaluate, and redesign the model as needed; design the cleanup; identify the constraints and trade-offs made in cleaning up an oil spill; and communicate the results.

Directions: Complete the following with information you have learned in this chapter.

1. Describe two different ways that oil is spilled in the oceans.

   _____

   _____

   _____

   _____

2. Describe some of the problems that you have to solve in cleaning up an oil spill.

   _____

   _____

   _____

   _____

   _____

   _____

3. Describe three constraints or trade-offs that you need to consider in cleaning up an oil spill.

   _____

   _____

   _____

   _____

   _____

   _____

Name: _____   Date: _____

4. Explain how an oil spill impacts the environment.

    _____

    _____

    _____

    _____

    _____

5. Explain how an oil spill impacts the wildlife in the environment.

    _____

    _____

    _____

    _____

Assessment of Technological Design

Directions: Fill in the form with the evidence from your oil spill cleanup plan.

Technological Design	Indicator	Evidence
Identified the problem	Problem was identified	
Identified a possible solution for the problem	List of brainstorming solutions was provided and one solution was identified to test	
Constructed a model and plan for their solution	Plan states specifically what materials to be used to clean up the spill and steps explaining how the materials will be used to clean up the spill	
Tested the model and plan	Plan and model were tested, data was recorded	
Evaluated the model/plan	Results of the data were analyzed and the plan/model was evaluated, problems with the plan were identified, solutions to the problems were identified	
Redesigned the model/ cleanup plan	Plan was redesigned to solve the identified problems in the first plan/model, and the new plan was tested and evaluated	
Identified constraints and trade-offs	3 constraints/trade-offs were described, and reasoning for trade-offs was explained	
Communicated the results	Presented plans and results to other students	

Chapter Three: Air-Powered Vehicles

Teacher Information

Topic: Air for Transportation

Standards:
NSES – Unifying Concepts and Processes
Evidence, Models, and Explanations
Form and Function

NSES – Content
NSES A: Science as Inquiry
NSES B: Physical Science
NSES E: Science and Technology

NCTM:
Problem Solving
Communication
Reasoning
Mathematical Connections
Statistics – Data collection and analysis
Measurement

ITEA:
Nature of Technology
Technology and Society
Understanding and Abilities in Engineering
Design

Concepts:
Air pressure
Mechanical energy from compressed air

Objectives:
Students will be able to…
- Explain how compressed air can be used to power vehicles.
- Describe how a hovercraft works.
- Explain how a compressed-air car works.
- Identify the advantages and disadvantages of compressed air cars.
- Explain that the energy from a compressed-air vehicle is renewable.

- Identify a problem; create a solution for the problem; construct, test, evaluate, and redesign the model as needed; identify the constraints and trade-offs made in using compressed air as an energy source, and communicate the results.

Activity One: Compressed-Air Hovercrafts (p. 34)
Materials: (for each group)
Discarded CD-ROM
Bottle top (pull-up type on drink or dish soap bottles)
Glue gun
9-inch balloons
meter sticks

Activity Two: Compressed-Air Car (p. 36)
Materials: (for each group)
3 x 5 index card
3 bendable straws
4 thread spools of the same size
tape
scissors
meter stick

TEACHER NOTE: This activity was adapted from a World In Motion activity called Jet Toy to fit the parameters of this book. For more information call 724-776-4841 or visit the World in Motion website: http://www.awim.org/curriculum/jettoy/

Educational Development Center, Inc. (2000) *A World in Motion: The Design Experience Challenge 1*. Warrendale, PA: Society of Automotive Engineers International.

Chapter Three: Air-Powered Vehicles

Student Information

Topic: Air for Transportation

Concepts:
Air pressure
Mechanical energy from compressed air

Objectives:
Students will be able to…
- Explain how compressed air can be used to power vehicles.
- Describe how a hovercraft works.
- Explain how a compressed-air car works.
- Identify the advantages and disadvantages of compressed-air cars.
- Explain that the energy from a compressed-air vehicle is renewable.
- Identify a problem; create a solution for the problem; construct, test, evaluate, and redesign the model as needed; identify the constraints and trade-offs made in using compressed air as an energy source, and communicate the results.

Content Background:

Jules Verne described a transportation system using compressed air in his book *Paris in the 21st Century*. In this book, Verne describes a society that was taken over by business and technology. He also describes trains and other machinery run by compressed air. Verne researched the science and technology

of the time to write his science fiction. Were his books predictions of the future, or were scientists, technologists, engineers, and mathematicians influenced by reading his imaginative tales?

Air-powered transportation is not new. By the end of the 19th century, street cars in Europe were powered by a simple pneumatic engine, which relied on heated air being forced through the engine. Air-powered pneumatic locomotives were popular in coal mines because the engines created no heat or spark, which meant they could not cause an explosion.

Pneumatic Locomotive

Many people experimented with compressed-air cars in the early 1920s. However, these vehicles did not go very far very fast, and further research and development may have been blocked by the oil industry.

In the 1950s, Christopher Cockerell invented the first hovercraft. A **hovercraft** is a vehicle that is traveling over a surface supported by a cushion of moving compressed air that pushes against the surface to lift the vehicle off of the surface. Hovercrafts can be simple like the one being constructed in this activity, or they can be an inflatable raft that can travel on land and water or a vehicle that flies.

Chapter Three: Air-Powered Vehicles

Student Information

Cockerell was an engineer who had an interest in boats and sailing. He read about Sir John Thornycroft, who tried to design and build a boat that could ride on a cushion of air so it could reduce the drag of the boat in the water. Thornycroft never succeeded in creating this boat.

Cockerell decided to try to solve the problem using the combustion engine that was not available to Thornycroft. His first hovercraft consisted of a smaller can inside of a larger can attached to a blower. The two cans lifted off of the ground. He later created a larger model that he called a hovercraft.

The engines in the hovercraft force air around the edge of the craft, creating a high-pressure ring of air. The ring of air pushed the hull of the boat up and circulated it under the hull to keep it up. It also kept the air from escaping. Current hovercrafts have a flexible skirt to help reduce the air loss.

Today, compressed-air vehicles are making giant developmental leaps. Motor Development International (MDI), a French company, is investigating compressed-air propulsion for automobiles. This is currently the only car that has atmospheric air as the only exhaust emission. The design uses a pair of air-driven pistons to turn a crankshaft that turns the wheels. The only heat from the engine comes from friction, and the engine can be made of lightweight aluminum.

Air cars have a top speed of 70 miles per hour and can travel 125 miles on flat roads before a refill is required. The compressed air is stored in carbon fiber tanks under the floor. Refilling can be done by a high-pressured air pump, home fueling device, or from an on-board compressor.

The main advantage of using a compressed-air vehicle is that it produces no pollution or greenhouse gases at the tailpipe. Another advantage is that, compared to gasoline costs, compressed air is quite cheap. Because the vehicles are lighter and smaller, so that they go farther and faster, they will also be somewhat cheaper to make and buy than regular cars.

While compressed-air cars produce no pollution at the tailpipe, energy must be used to compress the air, so they are not pollution-free vehicles. And because there are no compressed-air filling stations, drivers will only be able to go a few hundred miles, at most.

The first compressed-air vehicle commercially available is the Tata Motors model, available only in India. However, by 2011, there may be FlowAIR cars or MDI cars available in the United States.

In the following activities, you will be investigating the power of compressed air.

Tata Air-Compressed Car

Name: _____   Date: _____

Chapter Three: **Air-Powered Vehicles**

Student Activity

Activity One: Compressed-Air Hovercrafts

Question: Can compressed air be used to provide energy for transportation?

Materials:

Discarded CD-ROM   Bottle top (pull-up type that is on drink or dish soap bottles)
Glue gun   9-inch balloons
Meter sticks

Procedure:

1. Hot-glue the bottle top to the center of the CD. Let it dry.

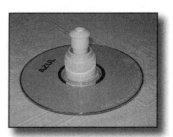

2. Push down to close the bottle top.

3. Inflate the balloon, and place the open end of the balloon over the top of the bottle top over the spout.

4. Put the craft on the table, pull open the bottle cap, and let go of the craft.

5. Observe and record what happens.

    _____

    _____

    _____

    _____

Name: _____   Date: _____

Chapter Three: Air-Powered Vehicles

Student Activity

Summary:

1. When I opened the bottle top and let go of the hovercraft…

   _____

   _____

   _____

   _____

   _____

2. Explain why this happens.

   _____

   _____

   _____

   _____

   _____

Challenge:

1. Design a hovercraft that will go in one direction.

2. Design a hovercraft that will move faster.

3. Design a hovercraft that will run on water and hard surfaces.

Name: _____ Date: _____

Chapter Three: Air-Powered Vehicles

Student Activity

Activity Two: Compressed-Air Car

Challenge Question: Can you design a car that is powered by the compressed air in a balloon?

Materials:

3 x 5 index card	3 bendable straws	4 thread spools of the same size
Tape	Scissors	Meter stick

Procedure:

1. Set up a racetrack that is at least 2 meters long and at least 1 meter wide on a flat surface.

Car Chassis Construction

2. Cut a 1 cm slit on the ends of the long sides of an index card 1 cm from the ends.
3. Fold the sides up 1 cm on all four sides of the card.
4. Overlap the corners and tape each corner.
5. You should have a box for a chassis.

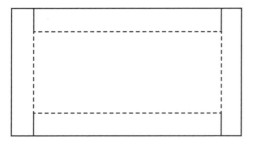 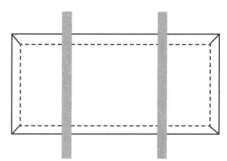

6. Turn the chassis over so the flat side is up, and tape a straw 1.5 cm from each end of the chassis for the axles on the flat side.
7. Put the spools on the ends of the straws.
8. Put tape on the ends of the straws to hold the spools on the axles, but make sure it does not stop the spools from turning on the straws.

Name: _____   Date: _____

Chapter Three: Air-Powered Vehicles

Student Activity

9. Turn the car over and see if the wheels turn freely. Make any needed adjustments
10. Cut the third straw 10 cm long with the bend in the middle.
11. Tape a balloon to one end of the straw so that the neck of the balloon is tightly sealed.
12. Attach the straw with the balloon to the top of the car 2 cm from the back of the car between the bend and the balloon.
13. Bend the straw slightly upward.
14. Blow on the straw to inflate the balloon, pinch off the straw, and set the car on a flat surface.
15. Let go of the straw.

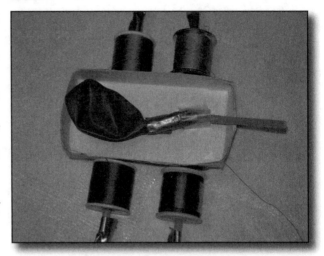

Observation:

Observe and record what happens.

_____

_____

_____

_____

_____

_____

Conclusion:

Explain what propels the car forward.

_____

_____

_____

_____

_____

Challenge:

1. Redesign the car to make it go faster.
2. Redesign the car to make it go farther.

Chapter Three: Air-Powered Vehicles

Further Investigation: Hovercrafts and Air Cars

Hovercrafts

Discover Hover
http://www.discoverhover.org/

Hoverclub of America
http://www.hoverclubofamerica.org/

The Hovercraft Museum Trust
http://www.hovercraft-museum.org/museum.html

Neoteric Hovercraft
http://www.neoterichovercraft.com/

Universal Hovercrafts
http://dev.hovercraft.com/content/

World Hovercraft Organization
www.worldhovercraft.org/

Air Cars

Gizmag.com: The Air Car
www.gizmag.com/go/7000/

Motor Development International
www.mdi.lu.english/

Squidoo: The Amazing Compressed-Air Car
www.squidoo.com/compressed-air-car

Zevolution
www.zevolution.com/

Books

Verne, Jules. (1996) *Paris in the Twentieth Century.* New York: Random House.

Name: _____ Date: _____

Chapter Three: Air-Powered Vehicles

Compressed Air Assessment

Objectives:

Students will be able to…

- Explain how compressed air can be used to power vehicles.
- Describe how a hovercraft works.
- Explain how a compressed-air car works.
- Identify the advantages and disadvantages of compressed-air cars.

1. Explain how compressed air can be used to power transportation.

   _____

   _____

   _____

   _____

   _____

   _____

2. Describe how a hovercraft works.

   _____

   _____

   _____

   _____

   _____

   _____

   _____

3. Explain how a compressed-air car works.

   _____

   _____

   _____

   _____

   _____

   _____

Name: _____ Date: _____

4.   Explain why the energy from compressed air is a renewable resource.

_____

_____

_____

_____

_____

_____

_____

_____

_____

_____

Assessment of Technological Design:

Directions: Fill in the chart with information about your hovercraft and air-car models.

Technological Design	Indicator	Evidence
Identified the problem	Problem was identified	
Identified a possible solution for the problem	List of brainstorming solutions was provided and one solution was identified to test	
Constructed a model and plan for the solution	Plan states specifically what materials to be used and steps explaining how the materials will be used	
Tested the model and plan	Plan and model were tested, data was recorded	
Evaluated the model/plan	Results of the data were analyzed and the plan/model was evaluated, problems with the plan were identified, solutions to the problems were identified	
Redesigned the model/plan	Plan was redesigned to solve the identified problems in the first plan/model, and the new plan was tested and evaluated	
Identified constraints and trade-offs	3 constraints/trade-offs were described, and reasoning for trade-offs was explained	
Communicated the results	Presented plans and results to other students	

Chapter Four: Air Power – Wind

Teacher Information

Topic: Wind Energy

Standards:
NSES – Unifying Concepts and Processes
Evidence, Models, and Explanations
Form and Function

NSES – Content
NSES A: Science as Inquiry
NSES B: Physical Science
NSES E: Science and Technology

NCTM:
Problem Solving
Communication
Reasoning
Mathematical Connections
Statistics – Data collection and analysis
Measurement
Geometry

ITEA:
Nature of Technology
Technology and Society
Understanding and Abilities in Engineering
Design

Concepts:
Wind energy
Uneven heating and cooling of the earth's surface
Placement of wind turbines
Renewable energy

Objectives:
Students will be able to…
- Identify a good location for a wind turbine around their school, based on the data collected.
- Explain why wind is a renewable energy source.
- Explain how wind energy can be turned into mechanical and electrical energy.
- Identify a problem; create a solution for the problem; construct, test, evaluate, and redesign the model as needed; identify the constraints and trade-offs made in using wind energy, and communicate the results.

Activity One: Wind Power (p. 44)
Materials: (for each group)
3-speed electric fan
5 x 8 cardstock or poster board for the boat hull
Hull pattern
Lightweight cardboard for the sails

Straw	Masking tape
Cellophane tape	Large paper clip
Scissors	Ballpoint pen
Ruler	3 meter sticks

TEACHER NOTE: This activity was adapted from a World In Motion activity called Skimmer to fit the parameters of this book. For more information, call 724-776-4841 or visit the World in Motion website: http://www.awim.org/curriculum/skimmer/

Educational Development Center, Inc. (2000) *A World in Motion: The Design Experience Challenge 1.* Warrendale, PA: Society of Automotive Engineers International.

Activity Two: Wind Turbines (p. 48)
Materials: (one set per team)
Disposable plates
New pencil with an eraser

Pushpin	Scissors
Markers	Rulers
Compass	Fan

Chapter Four: Air Power – Wind

Student Information

Topic: Wind Energy

Concepts:
Wind energy
Uneven heating and cooling of the earth's surface
Placement of wind turbines
Renewable energy

Objectives:
Students will be able to…
- Identify a good location for a wind turbine in their school based on the data collected.
- Explain why wind is a renewable energy source.
- Explain how wind energy can be turned into mechanical and electrical energy.
- Identify a problem; create a solution for the problem; construct, test, evaluate, and redesign the model as needed; identify the constraints and trade-offs made in using wind energy, and communicate the results.

Content Background:

Wind is air in motion. Wind is caused by the uneven heating and cooling of the earth's surface by the sun. During the day, air above the land heats more quickly than over water. The warm air over the land rises, and the cooler air over the water moves in to take its place (sea breezes). At night, air cools more rapidly over land than water, so the warm air over the water rises, and the cold air from the land moves in to take its place (land breezes). The wind in the atmosphere around the earth is created by air near the equator being heated more than air near the poles.

Wind power was used as early as 5000 B.C. to sail boats. The oldest windmills were used in China to pump water in 200 B.C. Persia and the Middle East used them to grind grains. In the 11th century in the Middle East, windmills were used mostly for food production. The Dutch used the windmill to drain lakes and marshes. American colonists used windmills to grind grain, pump water, and cut wood in sawmills. In the 19th century, farms used windmills to pump water and later to produce electricity for their homes.

Today, wind turbines can be found in many different places.

In the Ocean

Chapter Four: Air Power – Wind

Student Information

On Land

Scientists are again investigating how to use the wind to produce energy. The blades on the windmills, now called **wind turbines**, use the kinetic energy of the wind to turn. The blades are connected to an electric generator. The electric generator produces electricity to power something else. There are two types of wind turbines that generate electricity based on the direction of the rotating shaft—the vertical axis and the horizontal axis.

Vertical Axis Wind Turbine

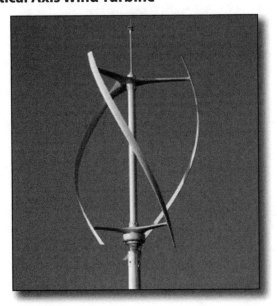

Horizontal Axis Wind Turbine

The advantages of using wind power are that it does not pollute the Earth and it is renewable. In areas where wind is fairly constant, wind power is an economical and clean power source. One problem with wind energy is that it only works when the wind is blowing. Other problems with the wind turbines are birds fly into them. Some people don't like the appearance or noise the turbines make.

Most of the wind power plants are in Europe and the United States. **Wind farms** are clusters of wind turbines in one location. They provide larger amounts of electricity than a single turbine. The largest wind farm is the Horse Hollow Wind Energy Center in Texas that has 421 wind turbines that generate enough electricity to power 220,000 homes.

Name: _____ Date: _____

Chapter Four: Air Power – Wind

Student Activity

Activity One: Wind Power

Question: Can a sailboat be designed to sail on a solid surface instead of water?

Materials:

    3-speed electric fan
    5 x 8 cardstock or poster board for the boat hull

Hull pattern	Lightweight cardboard for the sails	Straw
Masking tape	Cellophane tape	Large paper clip
Scissors	Ballpoint pen	Ruler
3 meter sticks		

Procedure:

1. Enlarge the hull pattern below so it is 20 cm long, and then cut out the pattern.

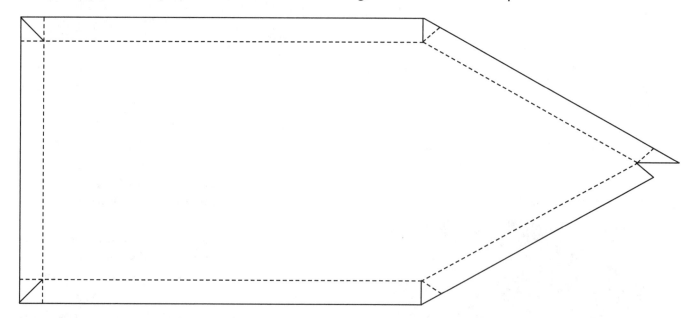

2. Cut the corners on the solid lines.
3. Use a ruler to score the dotted lines with a ballpoint pen.
4. Fold the edges up on the dotted lines.
5. Tape the corners.
6. On the inside of the boat, place three lengths of 14-cm-long masking tape.
7. On the center piece of tape, mark 0–12 centimeters in 2-cm intervals, starting with 0 at the stern (back) of the boat.
8. Pull the loops of the paper clip apart so the clip forms an L.

Name: _____ Date: _____

Chapter Four: Air Power – Wind

Student Activity

9. Attach the longer arm of the paper clip to the hull so that the other part is perpendicular to the skimmer.

10. Place the straw on the part of the paper clip that is standing up to form the mast of your boat.

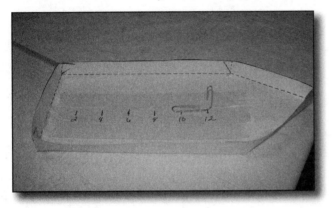 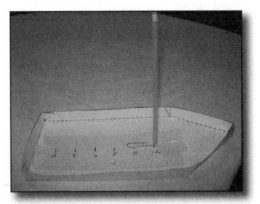

11. Design a sail from the piece of cardboard to go on the mast of the boat. The sail can be any shape you think will work.

12. Attach the sail to the mast.

13. Draw a picture of your sail design in the space below.

14. Set up a racetrack that is at least 3 meters long and at least 1 meter wide on a flat surface. Use masking tape to mark off the track starting line.

15. Put the 3-speed fan on one end of the table or track. Put tape on the track around three sides of the fan to keep it in the same place on the center of the track on each test.

16. Lay out three meter sticks end to end along the edge of the track so that you can measure the distance traveled.

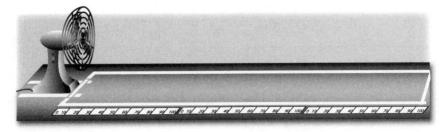

Name: _____   Date: _____

Chapter Four: Air Power – Wind

Student Activity

17. Place the back of your boat on the starting line.
18. Test the boat with the fan on low speed.
19. Record your observations and the distance traveled in the data table below.

Trial #	Fan Speed	Observations	Distance (cm)
1	Low Speed		
2	Low Speed		
3	Low Speed		
Average Distance at Low Speed			
1	Medium Speed		
2	Medium Speed		
3	Medium Speed		
Average Distance at Medium Speed			
1	High Speed		
2	High Speed		
3	High Speed		
Average Distance at High Speed			

Evaluation:

1. Describe what happened to your boat during the investigation, and explain why you think it happened.

   _____

   _____

   _____

   _____

   _____

   _____

   _____

   _____

   _____

Name: _____   Date: _____

Chapter Four: Air Power – Wind

Student Activity

2. Evaluate the design of your boat. Summarize your evaluation.

_____

_____

_____

_____

_____

_____

_____

_____

3. Make any appropriate modifications to your boat.
4. Test and evaluate your new design.
5. Once you have a boat that sails well, challenge the other teams' boats to a race.
6. Evaluate the design of your boat again after you see how the other boats sail.
7. Summarize your evaluation.

_____

_____

_____

_____

_____

_____

_____

_____

Challenge:

1. Redesign the boat/sail to make it sail farther.

2. Redesign the boat/ sail to make it go faster.

Name: _____ Date: _____

Chapter Four: Air Power – Wind

Student Activity

Activity Two: Wind Turbines

Challenge Question: Where is the best place to put a wind turbine to generate electricity at your school?

Materials: (one set per team)

Disposable plates	Fan
New pencil with an eraser	Pushpin
Scissors	Markers
Rulers	Compass

Procedure:

1. Draw lines to divide the paper plate into eight equal wedges.
2. Mark the center of the plate for the pushpin.
3. Mark a 3-cm circle in the center of the plate around the pushpin mark.
4. Cut the lines that divide the plate into eighths up to the 3-cm circle.

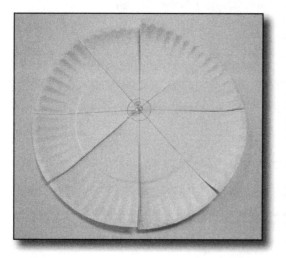 

5. Carefully bend and slightly twist the blades of your windmill.
6. Push the pushpin through the center of the plate and into the eraser end of the pencil. It should be loose enough so the propeller blades can spin.
7. Test it with the fan on medium and high speed to make sure it stays together and spins.
8. Record what happens to the windmill propeller when held in front of the fan.

_____

_____

_____

_____

Name: _____   Date: _____

Chapter Four: Air Power – Wind

Student Activity

9. You may have to adjust the blades or the position in front of the fan to make it spin. Record what adjustments you had to make in the blades to make it spin.

_____

_____

_____

_____

_____

10. Using your windmill, walk around the outside of your school and try to identify the best place to locate a wind turbine. Draw a diagram of your school.

11. Use a compass to identify the direction of your selected location and add it to your diagram.
12. Describe where you would put the wind turbine and why.

_____

_____

_____

_____

_____

Challenge:

1. Redesign your windmill to make it generate electrical current to run a small motor.

2. Redesign your windmill to make it more stable.

Chapter Four: Air Power – Wind

Further Investigation: Wind Power

Websites

How Stuff Works: How Wind Power Works
http://science.howstuffworks.com/wind-power7.htm

Kid Wind Project
http://www.kidwind.org/

NEED: Wind
http://www.need.org/needpdf/infobook_activities/IntInfo/WindI.pdf

U.S. Energy Information Administration: Energy Kids: Wind Energy
http://tonto.eia.doe.gov/kids/energy.cfm?page=wind_home-basics

Kits

Educational Innovations: Green Science Kits Windmill Generator
http://www.teachersource.com/Energy/AlternativeEnergy/GreenScienceKits.aspx

Fuel Cell Experiment Kit
http://www.kelvin.com/Merchant2/merchant.mv?Screen=PROD&Product_Code=283698

Horizon Fuel Cell Technology Kits
http://www.horizonfuelcell.com/

Wind Generator Kit
http://sciencekit.com/ig0019456/p/IG0019456/

Books

Kamkwamba, William and Brian Mealer. *The Boy Who Harnessed the Wind: Creating Currents of Electricity and Hope.* New York: Harper Collins Publishers. 2009.

Name: _____ Date: _____

Chapter Four: Air Power – Wind

Wind Energy Assessment

Objectives:

Students will be able to…
- Identify a good location for a wind turbine in their school based on the data collected.
- Explain why wind is a renewable energy source.
- Explain how wind energy can be turned into mechanical and electrical energy.
- Identify a problem; create a solution for the problem; construct, test, evaluate, and redesign the model as needed; identify the constraints and trade-offs made in using wind energy, and communicate the results.

1. Explain how wind can move a boat.

   _____

   _____

   _____

   _____

   _____

   _____

2. Explain how wind energy can make electricity.

   _____

   _____

   _____

   _____

   _____

   _____

3. Explain how to decide where a wind turbine should be placed.

   _____

   _____

   _____

   _____

   _____

   _____

   _____

Name: _____ Date: _____

4. Explain why wind energy is a renewable energy source.

_____

_____

_____

_____

_____

_____

_____

_____

_____

Assessment of Technological Design:

Directions: Fill in the chart with information about the models you made.

Technological Design	Indicator	Evidence
Identified the problem	Problem was identified	
Identified a possible solution for the problem	List of brainstorming solutions was provided and one solution was identified to test	
Constructed a model and plan for the solution	Plan states specifically what materials to be used and steps explaining how the materials will be used	
Tested the model and plan	Plan and model were tested, data was recorded	
Evaluated the model/plan	Results of the data were analyzed and the plan/model was evaluated, problems with the plan were identified, solutions to the problems were identified	
Redesigned the model/plan	Plan was redesigned to solve the identified problems in the first plan/model, and the new plan was tested and evaluated	
Identified constraints and trade-offs	3 constraints/trade-offs were described, and reasoning for trade-offs was explained	
Communicated the results	Presented plans and results to other students	

Chapter Five: Solar Power

Teacher Information

Topic: Solar Energy

Standards:
NSES – Unifying Concepts and Processes
Evidence, Models, and Explanations
Form and Function

NSES – Content
NSES A: Science as Inquiry
NSES B: Physical Science
NSES D: Earth Science
NSES E: Science and Technology
NSES F: Personal and Social Perspectives

NCTM:
Problem Solving
Communication
Reasoning
Mathematic Connections
Statistics – Data collection and analysis
Measurement
Geometry

ITEA:
Nature of Technology
Technology and Society
Understanding and Abilities in Engineering
Design

Concepts:
Solar energy
Photovoltaic cells
Solar thermal energy
Solar collectors
Renewable energy

Objectives:
Students will be able to…
- Explain what solar energy is.
- Explain how solar energy can be transformed to heat and electrical energy.

- Explain why solar energy is a renewable energy.
- Identify a problem; create a solution for the problem; construct, test, evaluate, and redesign the model as needed; identify the constraints and trade-offs made in using solar energy, and communicate the results.

Activity One: Solar Collector 1 (p. 57)
Materials: (for each group)
Four 8-oz. clear plastic cups
Black and white construction paper
400 mL cold water   4 thermometers
Plastic wrap   2 rubber bands
Scissors

Activity Two: Solar Collector 2—Cooker (p. 59)
Materials: (for each group)
Potato chip can with foil lining
Coat hanger
One 8 x 4-inch piece of transparency film or clear
     plastic report cover
1 hot dog per collector
Scissors   Exacto or utility knife
Tape   Tape measure
Nail

TEACHER NOTE: Adult supervision is needed when using the knife. Teachers may want to make the cuts before beginning the activity.

Activity Three: Photoelectric Cells (p. 63)
Materials: (for each group)
Solar car kit   Protractor
Masking tape   Meter sticks
Stopwatch

TEACHER NOTE: See Further Resources page for information about different solar car kits available for purchase.

Chapter Five: Solar Power

Student Information

Topic: Solar Energy

Concepts:
Solar energy
Photovoltaic cells
Solar thermal energy
Solar collectors
Renewable energy

Objectives:
Students will be able to…
- Explain what solar energy is
- Explain how solar energy can be transformed to heat and electrical energy.
- Explain why solar energy is a renewable energy.
- Identify a problem; create a solution for the problem; construct, test, evaluate, and redesign the model as needed; identify the constraints and trade-offs made in using solar energy, and communicate the results.

Content Background:

Solar energy is the radiant energy from the sun. It is found anywhere the sun shines and is a renewable resource. This energy can be converted into other forms of energy such as heat, light, and electricity. Two weeks of solar energy is equal to the potential (stored energy) in the world's entire supply of coal, oil, and gas. It is a non-polluting and

inexhaustible energy source. Scientists are developing new technologies to develop solar energy as a viable alternative to fossil fuels.

People have long used solar power. In ancient times, meat and fruits were dried in the sun. In 1767, Horace-Bénédict de Saussure made the first solar oven. The first solar furnace, invented by Antoine-Laurent Lavoisier, was so hot it melted a diamond. John Herschel, a British astronomer, created a device in 1830 to cook food using solar energy.

Solar energy can be converted to heat energy (thermal energy) by heating water used in homes, buildings, swimming pools, etc. It can also be used to heat spaces in homes, greenhouses, and other buildings. When the sun shines on the windows of your house or a greenhouse, the air in the house is warmed.

Solar energy can also be converted to electrical energy. **Photovoltaic cells** absorb light and convert it directly to electricity. This

energy can be used to run a motor or power electrical devices, such as calculators, watches, yard lights, stop signs, and toys. Larger systems can be used to power single homes or large power plants to produce electricity. Concentrating solar power plants use heat from thermal solar collectors to heat a fluid that produces steam used to drive an electrical generator.

There are three types of thermal power plants. The **parabolic power plant** uses large parabolic troughs that focus the sun's rays on a receiver pipe that tilts with the sun as it moves across

Chapter Five: Solar Power

Student Information

the sky. The trough can focus the sun's rays 30–100 times its normal intensity to create temperatures inside up to 750 degrees Fahrenheit.

A **solar dish** uses concentrating solar collectors that track the sun. The sun's energy is focused on the center of the dish. The solar dish's concentration ratio is 2,000 times the normal intensity of the sun, and the fluid temperature can reach 1,380 degrees Fahrenheit. The solar dish is attached to an engine that converts the heat energy into mechanical energy that turns an electrical generator to transform the mechanical energy to electrical energy.

The third type of thermal power plant is the **solar power tower**. Solar power towers focus concentrated solar energy on a heat exchanger. It uses flat mirrors (heliostats) to reflect the light on to a receiver. The energy is 1,500 times stronger than the sun.

One problem with using solar energy is that due to seasons, location, time of day, time of year, and weather, the amount of sunlight hitting the earth is not constant. Another problem using solar energy is that a large surface area is required to collect energy at a useful rate.

The investigations in this section introduce solar collectors of solar energy, the conversion of light energy into heat, and the use of photovoltaic cells to convert light energy directly into electrical energy.

Solar Trough

Solar Power Tower

Solar Dish

Name: _____   Date: _____

Chapter Five: Solar Power

Student Activity

Activity One: Solar Collector 1

Question: How does a solar collector work?

Adapted from Energy Exchange Newsletter (Nov. 2001) *Solar Collectors*. Manassas, VA: The National Energy Education and
    Development (N.E.E.D) Project

Materials:

Four 8-oz. clear plastic cups   Black and white construction paper
400 mL cold water   4 thermometers
Plastic wrap   2 rubber bands
Scissors

Procedure:

Solar collectors absorb radiant (solar) energy, convert it into heat, and store the heat (thermal energy). In this activity, you will be constructing and testing two solar collection systems. The water will be storing the thermal energy once it is converted from solar energy.

1. Cut two circles of white and two circles of black construction paper to fit the bottom of the plastic cups.
2. Place one circle in each of the four containers.
3. Cover each of the circles with 100 mL of cold water.
4. Record the temperature of the water in each cup in the data table on the next page.
5. Leave a thermometer in each container.
6. Cover one black and one white container with plastic wrap and hold it in place with the rubber bands.
7. Place all four containers in the sun so that the sun is directly over the container.
8. Let sit for 10 minutes and record the temperatures in the data table on the next page.

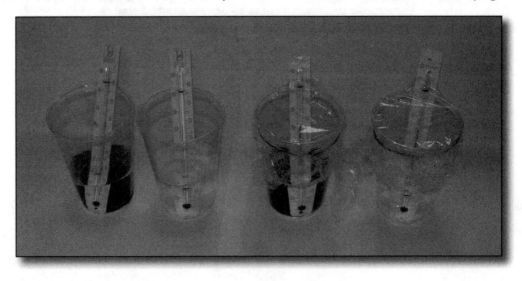

Name: _____ Date: _____

Chapter Five: Solar Power

Student Activity

Solar Collection Data Table:

	White No Cover	Black No Cover	White With Cover	Black With Cover
Starting temperature (C)				
Temperature (C) after 10 min.				
Change in temperature				

Conclusion:

1. Examine the data in your data table and summarize what you found out.

   _____

   _____

   _____

   _____

2. Which of the containers was the best design for a solar collector? Why was it the best?

   _____

3. Describe how the solar energy was transformed in this activity.

   _____

   _____

   _____

   _____

4. Describe how a solar collector works.

   _____

   _____

   _____

   _____

Challenge:

1. Redesign the solar collector to make it gather more solar energy.
2. Redesign the solar collector to make it better at storing heat.

Name: _____   Date: _____

Chapter Five: Solar Power

Student Activity

Activity Two: Solar Collector 2—Cooker

Challenge Question: Can you build a solar oven that will cook a hot dog with solar energy?

Materials:

Potato chip can with foil lining	Scissors
Exacto or utility knife	Tape
Coat hanger	Nail
One 8 x 4 inch piece of transparency film or clear plastic report cover	
1 hot dog per collector	Tape measure

Procedure:

Radiant energy (solar energy) from the sun can be reflected and concentrated on an object. Much of the radiant energy absorbed by an object is converted into thermal energy (heat). Radiant energy can pass through clear materials more easily than thermal energy. You are creating a solar collector like you made in the previous activity and using the hot dog to store the thermal energy.

1. Cut a coat hanger so that it will be 1 inch longer than the can on both ends. Leave the bend on one end of the coat hanger for a handle.

2. Cut a 7-inch slit down the long side of the potato chip can.
3. Cut a 3-inch slit across the potato chip can at both ends of the 7-inch slit.

Name: _____   Date: _____

Chapter Five: Solar Power

Student Activity

4.   Bend back the flaps created by the cuts on both sides.

5.   Cover the opening on the inside of the can with the clear plastic and tape the film into place. The top can be taped inside the can. The bottom may need to be taped on the outside.

6.   Make small holes large enough to hold the skewer tightly with the nail in the center of the metal end and the center of the plastic lid.

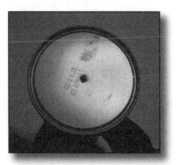

7.   Remove the lid.
8.   Place the skewer in the can, making sure the end of the coat hanger goes through the hole in the metal end of the can. Place the hot dog lengthwise on the skewer once the straight end is through the metal end of the can.
9.   Put the plastic lid on the can so that the other end of the skewer goes through the hole in the lid. The hot dog should now be suspended inside of the can.

Name: _____   Date: _____

Chapter Five: Solar Power

Student Activity

10.   Place the hot dog cooker in direct sunlight positioning the flaps so that they will reflect the radiant energy onto the hot dog. Remember, the angle of the incident light ray equals the angle of the reflected ray.

11.   How long will it take your hot dog to cook?

_____

12.   How will you know when the hot dog is cooked?

_____

13.   Time how long it takes to cook your hot dog.
14.   Check your hot dog at regular intervals
15.   Record your observations in the data table below. (Add more boxes as needed on your own paper.)

Cooking Time Data:

Time (min)	Observations

Name: _____ Date: _____

Chapter Five: Solar Power

Student Activity

16. Summarize your observations.

_____

_____

_____

_____

_____

Conclusion:

1. Was your prediction correct? Explain

_____

_____

_____

_____

2. How long did it take to cook your hot dog?

_____

_____

3. How did you know it was done?

_____

_____

_____

_____

Challenge:

1. Redesign the cooker to make it cook faster.
2. Redesign the cooker to insulate it to improve the energy efficiency.
3. Can you cook a hot dog using your solar collector with artificial light?

Name: _____ Date: _____

Chapter Five: Solar Power

Student Activity

Activity Three: Photoelectric Cells

Question: How is solar energy changed to electrical and mechanical energy?

Materials:

Solar car kit	Protractor
Masking tape	Meter sticks
Stopwatch	

Procedure:

1. Construct the solar car according to the kit instructions.

SunnySide Up Solar Car
photo courtesy Sun Wind Solar

2. Identify a sunny area outside with a smooth surface—a sidewalk, parking lot, etc.
3. Locate the sun. (Do not stare directly into the sun.)
4. Predict the angle to set the solar panel on the car to get the maximum exposure to the sun.
5. Measure the angle of the solar panel.
6. Record the angle measurement.
7. Set the panel and place the car on the starting line.
8. Record your observations, the distance traveled, angle of panel, direction the panel was facing, and time of day in the data table below.

Data Table Trial 1:

Time	Distance (m)	Direction of Solar Panel	Angle of Solar Panel	Observations
			Prediction	
			Actual	

Name: _____ Date: _____

Chapter Five: Solar Power

Student Activity

9. Make any necessary adjustments to make the car go in a straight line.
10. Record the adjustments made.

_____

_____

_____

11. Make any necessary adjustments to the solar panel to get the maximum exposure to the sun to make the car go farther.
12. Record the adjustments made.

_____

_____

_____

13. Set the panel and place the car on the starting line.
14. Record your observations in the data table below.

Data Table Trial 2:

Time	Distance (m)	Direction of Solar Panel	Angle of Solar Panel	Observations

Conclusion:

How did the design changes affect the car?

_____

_____

_____

_____

_____

Challenge:

1. Redesign the car to make the car move faster.
2. Redesign the car to make it go farther.

Chapter Five: Solar Power

Further Investigation: Solar Power

Articles

Dillow, C. (2010) "System Stores Wind and Solar Power in the Form of Natural Gas, to Fit Neatly into Existing Infrastructure."
http://www.popsci.com/science/article/2010-05/carbon-neutral-natural-gas-made-wind-and-solar-could-power-existing-infrastructures

Hsu, J. (2009) "Scaly BMW Concept Car Collects Solar Power, Then Raises Panels to Brake."
http://www.popsci.com/cars/article/2009-10/bmw-concept-car-harnesses-solar-scale-air-brakes

Locke, S. (2009) "China Plans World's Largest Solar Power Plant."
http://www.popsci.com/scitech/article/2009-09/biggest-solar-power-plant-set-

The New York Times. (2009) "U.S. Solar Firm Cracks Chinese Market."
http://green.blogs.nytimes.com/2009/09/08/china-signs-deal-with-first-solar/

Roberts, D. (2009) "Solar Power: Harnessing the Terawatts of Energy We Get From the Sun."
http://www.popsci.com/environment/article/2009-06/solar-power

Sato, Shigeru, and Yugi Okada. (2009) "Mitsubishi, IHI to Join $21 Bln Space Solar Project (Update1)."
http://bloomberg.com/apps/news?pid=newsarchive&sid=aJ5291/

Books

Gould, A. (1986) *Great Explorations in Math and Science: Hot Water and Warm Homes From Sunlight.* Berkley, CA: GEMS.

Websites

How Stuff Works
http://science.howstuffworks.com/solar-cell1.htm

NASA: Life in a Greenhouse
http://spaceplace.jpl.nasa.gov/en/kids/tes/gases/

NEED Global Climate Change
http://www.need.org/needpdf/infobook_activities/SecInfo/Global.pdf

NEED Solar Energy Info book
http://www.need.org/needpdf/infobook_activities/IntInfo/SolarI.pdf

Pizza Box Oven
http://txu-solaracademy.need.org/Pizza Box Solar Oven.pdf

Raw Solar
http://raw-solar.com/

U.S. Department of Energy: Technologies: Photovoltaics
http://www1.eere.energy.gov/solar/photovoltaics.html

U.S. Energy Information Administration: Solar
http://tonto.eia.doe.gov/kids/energy.cfm?page=solar_home-basics

Chapter Five: Solar Power

Further Investigation: Solar Power

Solar Kits

Educational Innovations: Multi Project Solar Kit
http://www.teachersource.com/Energy/
AlternativeEnergy/MultiProjectSolarKit.aspx

Educational Innovations: Solar Cells
http://www.teachersource.com/Ultraviolet/
SolarEnergy/SolarCells.aspx

Educational Innovations: Solar Tube
http://www.teachersource.com/AirPressure/
RocketsAndBalloons/SolarTube.aspx

Horizon Fuel Cell Technology Kits
http://www.horizonfuelcell.com/

NEED: Solar Kit
http://www.need.org/needpdf/Exploring
SolarTeacher.pdf

Northwestern Nature Shop: The Solar Car Book and Kit
http://www.northwestnatureshop.com/Toys_
and_Games/Toys_by_Brand/Solar_Car_Kits/294.
html

Science Kit: Solar Electricity Kit
http://sciencekit.com/solar-electricity-kit/p/
IG0024377/

Siliconsolar
http://www.siliconsolar.com/solarpowered-cars.
html

Solar Energy Kit Science Kit
http://sciencekit.com/solar-energy-kit/p/
IG0022499/

Solar Home: Mini Solar Robot Kit
http://www.solarhome.org/minisolarrobotkit-
supersolarracingcar.aspx

Solar Panel Kits Science Kit
http://sciencekit.com/solar-panel-kit/p/
IG0024378/

Solar Racers
www.kelvin.com/Merchant2/merchant.
mv?Screen=CTGY&Store_Code=K&Category_
Code=TRLASR

Sun Wind Solar
http://www.sunwindsolar.com/a_scripts/
n_educational_kits.php

Thames and Kosmos: Power House
http://www.thamesandkosmos.com/products/
ph/ph2.html

World's Largest Solar Bag Science Kit
http://sciencekit.com/worldand%238217%3Bs-
largest-solar-bag/p/IG0027392/

Name: _____   Date: _____

Chapter Five: Solar Power

Solar Power Assessment

Objectives:

Students will be able to…

- Explain what solar energy is.
- Explain how solar energy can be transformed to another form of energy.
- Identify a problem; create a solution for the problem; construct, test, evaluate, and redesign the model as needed; identify the constraints and trade-offs made in using solar energy, and communicate the results.

Solar Energy Matching:

_____ 1.   Solar Collector

a. 3 types—parabolic, solar dish, solar power tower

_____ 2.   Radiant Energy

b. Heat energy

_____ 3.   Thermal Energy

c. Solar energy from the sun

_____ 4.   Photovoltaic Cell

d. A device that absorbs radiant energy, converts it into heat energy, and stores it

_____ 5.   Thermal Power Plants

e. A device that converts solar energy directly into electrical energy

6.   Describe three examples of solar heating.

_____

_____

_____

_____

_____

_____

7.   Explain how a photovoltaic cell works.

_____

_____

_____

_____

_____

Name: _____   Date: _____

8.   Explain how a solar collector works.

_____

_____

_____

_____

9.   Describe two disadvantages of using solar energy.

_____

_____

_____

10.   Is solar energy a renewable resource? Explain.

_____

_____

_____

Assessment of Technological Design:
Directions: Fill in the chart with information about the models you made.

Technological Design	Indicator	Evidence
Identified the problem	Problem was identified	
Identified a possible solution for the problem	List of brainstorming solutions was provided and one solution was identified to test	
Constructed a model and plan for the solution	Plan states specifically what materials to be used and steps explaining how the materials will be used	
Tested the model and plan	Plan and model were tested, data was recorded	
Evaluated the model/plan	Results of the data were analyzed and the plan/model was evaluated, problems with the plan were identified, solutions to the problems were identified	
Redesigned the model/plan	Plan was redesigned to solve the identified problems in the first plan/model, and the new plan was tested and evaluated	
Identified constraints and trade-offs	3 constraints/trade-offs were described, and reasoning for trade-offs was explained	
Communicated the results	Presented plans and results to other students	

Chapter Six: Biomass

Teacher Information

Topic: Biomass – Fermentation of Plant Matter

Standards:
NSES – Unifying Concepts and Processes
Evidence, Models, and Explanations
Change, Constancy, and Measurement
Form and Function

NSES – Content
NSES A: Science as Inquiry
NSES B: Physical Science
NSES C: Life Science
NSES E: Science and Technology

NCTM:
Problem Solving
Communication
Reasoning
Statistics – Data collection and analysis
Measurement
Geometry

ITEA:
Nature of Technology
Technology and Society
Understanding and Abilities in Engineering
Design

Concepts:
Biomass
Photosynthesis
Renewable energy

Objectives:
Students will be able to…
- Define biomass.
- Explain that biomass receives its energy from the sun.
- Explain what renewable energy is.
- Describe how biomass energy is used.
- Explain that bacteria cause decomposition of grass, which causes the biomass to change to heat and chemical energy.
- Identify a problem; create a solution for the problem; construct, test, evaluate, and redesign the model as needed; identify the constraints and trade-offs made in using biomass as an energy source, and communicate the results.

Activity: Biomass (p. 71)

Materials: (for each group)
  Black trash bag
  Wire tie
  Grass clippings
  Thermometer
  Rubber gloves

Chapter Six: Biomass

Student Information

Topic: Biomass – Fermentation of Plant Matter

Concepts:
Biomass
Photosynthesis
Renewable energy

Objectives:
Students will be able to…
- Define biomass.
- Explain that biomass receives its energy from the sun.
- Explain what renewable energy is.
- Describe how biomass energy is used.
- Explain that bacteria cause decomposition of grass, which causes the biomass to change to heat and chemical energy.
- Identify a problem; create a solution for the problem; construct, test, evaluate, and redesign the model as needed; identify the constraints and trade-offs made in using biomass as an energy source, and communicate the results.

Content Background:

Biomass is organic matter. At one time, it was a living thing. Biomass is carbon based, which can be used as an energy source. Biomass is a renewable energy source, which means that it can be replenished in a short period of time. Examples of biomass are wood, crops, grasses, and plant and animal wastes.

Throughout history, humans have used biomass for energy to heat their homes and cook their food. Early fuels included wood, grass, and animal dung.

The energy stored in the biomass is from the sun, captured through photosynthesis. **Photosynthesis** is a plant process that takes in carbon dioxide and water in the presence of sunlight to make glucose (sugar) and oxygen. Plants use sunlight, air, water, and nutrients from the soil to make glucose. The

chemical energy in the plants is passed on to the animals that eat them, so plants provides energy for many other living things.

The formula for photosynthesis is.

$$water + carbon\ dioxide + sunlight = glucose\ and\ oxygen$$

or

$$6H_2O + 6CO_2 + radiant\ energy = C_6H_{12}O_6 + 6O_2$$

There are different ways that biomass can be converted to other forms of usable energy. Biomass is converted to another form of energy by burning, bacterial decay, fermentation, and conversion to gas or liquid fuels, such as ethanol or biodiesel. Wood and other plants, animal wastes, and garbage can be burned to generate steam and electricity.

Bacterial decay produces methane gas when bacteria feed on dead plants and animals. Methane gas is the main ingredient in natural gas.

Chapter Six: Biomass

Student Information

Methane gas can be burned to produce heat or electricity. Some landfills are drilled to capture the methane gas given off by the breakdown of the garbage.

Fermentation of crops like corn and sugar cane can produce **ethanol**, which is a form of alcohol that can be used for motor fuel. It is mixed with gasoline to lower the carbon monoxide emissions from a car. E85 fuel is a gasoline blend that is 85 percent ethanol, which is sometimes made from corn.

Biodiesel can be produced from leftover food products like vegetable oils and animal fats, or it can be made from crops such as soybeans.

Biomass currently accounts for only four percent of the energy used in the United States. Two percent of the energy we use today is from wood and wood wastes, such as bark, sawdust, wood chips, and wood scrap. Ten percent of the total biomass used in the United States comes from municipal solid waste—in other words, garbage. Waste-to-energy plants burn garbage to make steam and electricity. Biogas—methane—can also be collected from decaying landfills. Farmers also use animal wastes in tanks called "digesters" that convert the wastes into methane gas.

The major advantage of disposing of wastes this way is it reduces the amount of garbage. It is also a virtually unlimited resource. However, it is actually more cost-effective to generate electricity using coal, nuclear, or hydropower plants than garbage.

Problems with waste-to-energy plants that burn the garbage include controlling the air pollution caused by burning the waste and disposing of the ash. The Environmental Protection Agency (EPA) requires scrubbers, filters, and electrostatic precipitators to clean the air. The ash may contain high levels of metals, such as lead and cadmium. Batteries are the largest source of lead and cadmium in landfills. About one-third of the ash is used in landfills as a daily or final cover layer, to build roads, make cement blocks, or make artificial reefs.

Another disadvantage of using biomass is that it pollutes the air with the greenhouse gas carbon dioxide when it burns. However, it produces less carbon dioxide than fossil fuels because when biomass crops grow, they remove almost the same amount of carbon dioxide in photosynthesis as they put out when they are burned.

Scientists, researchers, and engineers are investigating new ways to use more biomass and less fossil fuel to cut back on wastes and reduce greenhouse gases. **Biofuels** convert biomass into liquid fuels for transportation. **Bio-power** is burning biomass directly or converting it to gas or liquid fuels that burn more efficiently. **Bio-products** convert biomass into chemicals for plastics and other products that are typically made from petroleum.

In this investigation, you will demonstrate the bacterial decomposition of the biomass grass to convert the sun's energy into other forms of energy.

Name: _____ Date: _____

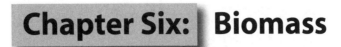
Chapter Six: Biomass

Student Activity

Activity: Biomass

Energy can be retrieved or converted from biomass by decomposition. This activity will demonstrate bacterial decomposition. The energy from the sun in the grass is converted to heat and chemical energy. The decomposed grass may be used as compost for the garden to put nutrients from the grass back into the soil.

Materials:

Black trash bag   Wire tie
Grass clippings   Thermometer
Rubber gloves

Procedure:

1. Place the grass clippings in the black garbage bag.
2. Record your observations of the grass clippings and the starting temperature in the data table.
3. Close the bag with the tie.
4. Place the bag outside in a location that gets several hours of daily sunlight for two weeks.
5. Check the bag daily and record observations and the temperature of the grass.

Grass Data:

Day	Temperature (C)	Observations of the Grass
1		
2		
3		
4		
5		
6		

Name:_____   Date:_____

Chapter Six: Biomass

Student Activity

Day	Temperature (C)	Observations of the Grass
7		
8		
9		
10		
11		
12		
13		
14		

6.   Summarize your observations._____

_____

_____

_____

Conclusion:

Explain what caused changes to the grass by the end of the second week.

_____

_____

_____

Challenge:

1.   Redesign the investigation to make the grass decompose faster.
2.   Redesign the investigation to make the grass convert more energy from the grass.

Chapter Six: Biomass

Further Investigation: Biomass Energy

Websites

Biomass Energy Resource Center
http://www.biomasscenter.org/

Biomass Magazine
http://www.biomassmagazine.com/

Biomass One: Renewable Energy
http://www.biomassone.com/

Biomass Power Association
http://www.usabiomass.org/

Energy Justice Network Fact Sheet: Biomass Incineration
http://www.energyjustice.net/biomass/

Green Jobs
http://www.greenjobs.com/Public/info/
industry_background.aspx?id=13

Iowa Public Television: Explore More–The Future of Energy: Biomass
http://www.iptv.org/exploremore/energy/
profiles/biomass.cfm

National Renewable Energy Laboratory: Biomass Research: Learning About Renewable Energy
http://www.nrel.gov/learning/re_biomass.html

NEED Biomass
http://www.need.org/needpdf/infobook_
activities/IntInfo/BiomassI.pdf

Natural Resources Defense Council: Renewable Energy for America
http://www.nrdc.org/energy/renewables/
biomass.asp

Power Scorecard Electricity From Biomass
http://www.powerscorecard.org/tech_detail.
cfm?resource_id=1

Pure Energy Systems
http://peswiki.com/energy/Directory:Biomass

Thinkquest: Alternative Energy Resources
http://library.thinkquest.org/06aug/01335/
biomass.htm

U.S. Department of Energy: Biomass Program
http://www1.eere.energy.gov/biomass/

U.S Department of Energy: Energy Efficiency and Renewable Energy
http://www.eere.energy.gov/

U.S. Department of Energy: Energy Empowers
http://www.energyempowers.gov/category/
Biomass.aspx

U.S. Energy Information Administration: Energy Kids: Biofuels
http://www.eia.doe.gov/kids/energy.cfm?
page=biofuel_home-basics

U.S. Energy Information Administration: Energy Kids: Biomass
http://www.eia.doe.gov/kids/energy.
cfm?page=biomass_home-basics

Union of Concerned Scientists: Citizens and Scientists for Environmental Solutions
http://www.ucsusa.org/clean_energy/
technology_and_impacts/energy_
technologies/how-biomass-energy-works.html

Washington State Department of Natural Resources: Forest Biomass
http://www.dnr.wa.gov/ResearchScience/
Topics/OtherConservationInformation/Pages/
em_biomass.aspx

Name: _____ Date: _____

Chapter Six: Biomass

Biomass Assessment

Objectives:

Students will be able to…

- Define biomass.
- Explain that biomass receives its energy from the sun.
- Explain what renewable energy is.
- Describe how biomass energy is used.
- Explain that bacteria cause decomposition of grass, which causes the biomass to change to heat and chemical energy.
- Identify a problem; create a solution for the problem; construct, test, evaluate, and redesign the model as needed; identify the constraints and trade-offs made in using biomass as an energy source, and communicate the results.

Matching:

_____ 1. Biomass

_____ 2. Fermentation

_____ 3. Biodiesel

_____ 4. Bacterial decay

_____ 5. Waste-to-energy plant

a. Organic matter that can be used to produce energy

b. Fuel made from the oil of plants

c. Process of producing ethanol from corn and sugar cane

d. Process that produces methane gas from dead plants and animals

e. Makes steam and electrical energy by burning garbage

6. Explain how grass clippings can be used as a renewable energy source.

_____

_____

_____

_____

_____

_____

_____

Name: _____   Date: _____

7. Design a system that will use the energy from grass clippings to provide energy for something else.

_____

_____

_____

_____

_____

_____

_____

_____

Assessment of Technological Design:
Directions: Fill in the chart with information about your model composter.

Technological Design	Indicator	Evidence
Identified the problem	Problem was identified	
Identified a possible solution for the problem	List of brainstorming solutions was provided and one solution was identified to test	
Constructed a model and plan for the solution	Plan states specifically what materials to be used and steps explaining how the materials will be used	
Tested the model and plan	Plan and model were tested, data was recorded	
Evaluated the model/plan	Results of the data were analyzed and the plan/model was evaluated, problems with the plan were identified, solutions to the problems were identified	
Redesigned the model/plan	Plan was redesigned to solve the identified problems in the first plan/model, and the new plan was tested and evaluated	
Identified constraints and trade-offs	3 constraints/trade-offs were described, and reasoning for trade-offs was explained	
Communicated the results	Presented plans and results to other students	

Chapter Seven: Hydrogen Fuel Cells

Teacher Information

Topic: Car Design/Hydrogen/Hydrogen Fuel Cells

Standards:

NSES – Unifying Concepts and Processes
Evidence, Models, and Explanations
Change, Constancy, and Measurement
Form and Function

NSES – Content
NSES A: Science as Inquiry
NSES B: Physical Science
NSES D: Earth Science
NSES E: Science and Technology

NCTM:

Problem Solving	Communication
Reasoning	Measurement Geometry

Statistics – Data collection and analysis

ITEA:

Nature of Technology   Technology and Society
Understanding and Abilities in Engineering Design

Concepts:

Force – inertia, gravity, friction, air resistance/drag
Aerodynamics   Engines
Car design   Movement of cars
Fuel cell design and how it functions
Fuel cell cars

Objectives:

Students will be able to…

- Identify the forces that affect the movement of a car and how these forces can be overcome.
- Explain how a car works.
- Explain the function of the chassis, wheel and axle, engine, fuel, etc.
- Identify a problem; create a solution for the problem; construct, test, evaluate, and redesign the model as needed; identify the constraints and trade-offs made in using hydrogen as an energy source, and communicate the results.

Activity One: Car Design (p. 79)
Materials: (for each group)
2 toy cars per group (variety of different body styles, masses, etc.)
Meter stick   Stopwatch
Masking tape   Ruler
Double pan or triple-beam balance

Activity Two: Electrolysis (p. 83)
Materials: (for each group)
100 mL warm water   2 mL salt
6-volt lantern battery (do not use any larger)
2 sets of alligator clips (one red, one black)
Large metal paper clips
1 clear plastic dish that will hold 120 mL water
Safety goggles
TEACHER NOTE: This activity MUST be closely supervised.

Activity Three: Fuel Cell Car (p. 85)
Materials: (for each group)
Fuel cell car kit   Masking tape
Meter sticks
TEACHER NOTE: This activity MUST be closely supervised. Read and follow all safety precautions.

Two sources for fuel cell cars include:
Thames and Kosmos – Fuel Cell Car Kit - Solar Cell provides electricity for the electrolysis
http://www.thamesandkosmos.com/products/fc/fc2.html

World In Motion Fuel Cell Cars - Society of Automotive Engineers – 2 AA Batteries provide the power for the electrolysis.
http://www.awim.org/curriculum/fuelcell/

The World in Motion Fuel Cell Kit is a three-week unit introducing students to the car chassis design, the concepts of fuel cell technology, production of hydrogen from the fuel cell, and using the fuel cell to power a car.

Chapter Seven: Hydrogen Fuel Cells

Student Information

Topic: Car Design/Hydrogen/
Hydrogen Fuel Cells

Concepts:
Force – inertia, gravity, friction, air resistance/drag
Aerodynamics
Engines
Car design
Movement of cars
Fuel cell design and how it functions
Fuel cell cars

Objectives:
Students will be able to…
- Identify the forces that affect the movement of a car and how these forces can be overcome.
- Explain how a car works.
- Explain the function of the chassis, wheel and axle, engine, fuel, etc.
- Identify a problem; create a solution for the problem; construct, test, evaluate, and redesign the model as needed; identify the constraints and trade-offs made in using hydrogen as an energy source, and communicate the results.

Content Background:

The automotive industry has used a variety of chassis designs for cars and trucks based on the needs of the consumer. The current body styles include: SUV, minivan, van, pickup truck, station wagon, sedan, coupe, etc.

The body design on a race car is different than a car for a family of six. The purpose of the two cars is different. Race cars are designed for speed. These cars are aerodynamic, made of lightweight materials, and have engines that are specially designed to provide the power needed for high speed.

Minivans, wagons, trucks, and vans are designed to carry larger families or to haul things.

These vehicles have engines built to provide hauling power. They do not get the gas mileage of the smaller cars because they are larger and heavier.

Smaller cars and hybrid cars are designed for driving fewer people, hauling fewer things, and some are more fuel-efficient. Hybrid cars are designed to be more fuel-efficient and to be less polluting. They use both gasoline and electricity as the fuel source. They usually switch over from the electric battery to the gas engine so that the driver does not realize the power sources have switched.

Because they are focused on fuel efficiency, they are usually made of lighter weight materials and smaller engines.

All of the cars discussed so far use gasoline as the fuel source. New sources of fuel for the automotive industry include compressed air, hydrogen, and biofuels.

Hydrogen is the simplest element. It is colorless, odorless, tasteless, is slightly soluble in water, and is highly explosive. It is the most abundant gas in the universe, and it usually exists combined with another hydrogen atom. The energy in the sun and other stars comes from hydrogen.

Hydrogen atoms combine to form helium by a process called fusion. **Fusion** is when two or more nuclei are joined (fused) together to form a new substance. The fusion reaction of the hydrogen in our sun gives off the radiant energy that gives us light, makes the wind blow, and the rain fall. This energy is stored in the fossil fuels we currently use.

Pure hydrogen is not found on Earth because it is lighter than air, so it rises and is ejected

Chapter Seven: Hydrogen Fuel Cells

Student Information

from the atmosphere. On Earth, hydrogen mixes with other elements to form compounds like water, methane gas, coal, petroleum, and biomass. It is the most abundant element in the Earth's crust.

Hydrogen has the highest energy content of any common fuel by weight, but the lowest by volume. Hydrogen can be extracted from water, fossil fuels, or biomass and produced as a by-product of chemical reactions. The most common ways to produce hydrogen are steam reforming and electrolysis. Some algae and bacteria also give off hydrogen.

Steam reforming is used by many industries to produce hydrogen. In this process, methane is separated into hydrogen and carbon atoms. However, this process results in greenhouse gas emissions that contribute to global warming.

Electrolysis is a process that splits a water molecule by running an electric current through it. This process splits water molecules to produce hydrogen and oxygen gases. There are no emissions, but it is an expensive process. The hydrogen gas that is produced can be used in a fuel cell to power a vehicle. When the fuel cell operates, the hydrogen and oxygen are recombined (burned), and the energy released can turn a generator or electric motor. Small fuel cells can power an electric car, or large ones can provide electricity for remote areas.

Hydrogen vehicles are electric vehicles that carry hydrogen as a liquid or a gas fuel. The engine converts the hydrogen into electrical energy to move the vehicle. In 2010, there were only 200 to 300 hydrogen-fueled vehicles—buses and

cars. Only a few of these vehicles burn the hydrogen directly instead of converting the energy from the hydrogen into electricity to run the electric motor. Burning the hydrogen directly produces almost no pollution because the by-product of the combustion is water.

One of the challenges in developing alternative energy sources for transportation is having the infrastructure in place to make the new source practical. There are gas stations in every town and on every road. However, only a few locations have hydrogen refueling stations already set up.

The dilemma for any new fuel source is having some way of refueling the car in multiple places. Until the cars are in use, there is no need for the new type of fueling stations. No one will purchase the car until the stations are built, and no one wants to spend the money to build a new type of fuel station when no one owns the vehicles that use it.

Another challenge of using hydrogen as a fuel source is the safe transportation and storage of hydrogen. Hydrogen ignites in the air at very low concentrations and could be sparked by static electricity.

Hydrogen is a clean, renewable source of energy, but it currently is not cost-effective to use. The pros and cons of using hydrogen as an energy source must be weighed before a decision is made.

The activities in this section examine car design and fuel efficiency, form and function of vehicles, and introduce students to fuel cell technology.

Name: _____   Date: _____

Chapter Seven: Hydrogen Fuel Cells

Student Activity

Activity One: Car Design

Challenge Question: What forces are acting on a car?

Materials:
  2 toy cars per group (variety of different body styles, masses, etc.)
  Meter stick   Stopwatch   Masking tape
  Double pan or triple-beam balance   Ruler

Procedure:
  1. Select two cars.
  2. Closely examine each car.
  3. Record your observations of the parts of each car in the data table below.
  4. Use the balance to find the mass of the car.
  5. Record the mass in the data table below

	Car 1	Car 2
Description of Chassis		
Mass of car (g)		
Type of Wheels		
Describe how the car moves		

  6. Roll the car across the floor.
  7. Record your observations below.

Car 1 Observations	Car 2 Observations

Name: _____   Date: _____

Chapter Seven: Hydrogen Fuel Cells

Student Activity

8. What made the car roll across the floor?

_____

_____

9. How do the wheels help the car move?

_____

_____

_____

10. How does the body style affect how the car moves?

_____

_____

_____

11. Use masking tape to mark out a track for your cars 1 m wide and 4 m long.
12. Mark the starting line on the center of one end of the track.
13. Push your car so that you release the car on the front edge of the starting line of the track.
14. Record the distance the car rolls in meters and how long it took it to stop in seconds.
15. Do three trials for each car.

According to **Newton's Law of Inertia**, an object in motion stays in motion at a constant speed in the same direction until acted upon by another force, and an object at rest stays at rest unless acted upon by another force. A **force** is defined as a push or pull on an object. Inertia is one of the forces that may be acting on the car. Drag or air resistance, friction, gravity, and energy to get the car started are also forces that could be acting on the car.

16. Identify what forces were acting on the car and record it in the data table.

Car Roll Data Table:

Car 1	Distance (m)	Time (sec)	Observations	Forces – gravity, inertia, friction, drag
Trial 1				
Trial 2				
Trial 3				

Name: _____ Date: _____

Chapter Seven: Hydrogen Fuel Cells

Student Activity

Car 2	Distance (m)	Time (sec)	Observations	Forces – gravity, inertia, friction, drag
Trial 1				
Trial 2				
Trial 3				

Conclusion:

1. From your observations, describe the parts of the car that help it move.

_____

_____

_____

_____

_____

2. What parts make a real car move?

_____

_____

_____

_____

_____

_____

3. How do the size of the car and shape of the car affect how the car moves?

_____

_____

_____

_____

_____

_____

Name: _____   Date: _____

Chapter Seven: Hydrogen Fuel Cells

Student Activity

4. Why do some cars need larger or more powerful engines than others?

    _____

    _____

    _____

    _____

5. How would you redesign the cars to counteract the forces that are acting on them?

    _____

    _____

    _____

    _____

    _____

6. Draw a diagram of your designs.

Challenge:
1. On your own paper, make a drawing of how you would redesign the cars that you have to make them move farther.
2. On your own paper, make a drawing of how you would redesign the cars that you have to make them move faster.

Name: _____   Date: _____

Chapter Seven: Hydrogen Fuel Cells

Student Activity

Activity Two: Electrolysis

Challenge Question: How can you make hydrogen from water?

Materials:

      100 mL warm water   2 mL salt
      6-volt lantern battery – do not use anything larger
      2 sets of alligator clips – one red, one black
      Large metal paper clips
      1 clear plastic dish that will hold 120 mL of water
      Safety goggles

NOTE TO TEACHER: This activity MUST be closely supervised.

    Water molecules have two atoms of hydrogen and one atom of oxygen. Electrolysis is a process that passes an electrical current through water to separate the hydrogen and the oxygen atoms. This investigation will demonstrate the process of electrolysis.

Procedure:

1. Dissolve the salt in the water.
2. Bend the paper clips so that one piece is sticking up.
3. Connect the red alligator clip to the positive terminal of the battery.
4. Connect the black alligator clip to the negative terminal of the battery.
5. Connect the other end of each alligator clip to a paper clip
6. Place the paper clips in the water so that the alligator clips are not touching the water

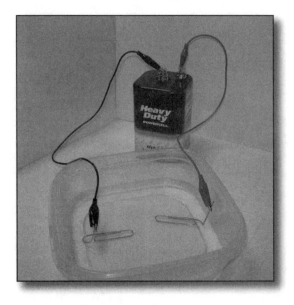

Name: _____ Date: _____

Chapter Seven: Hydrogen Fuel Cells

Student Activity

7. Record your observations of the paper clips in the data table below.

Electrolysis Data Table:

Clip	Terminal	Observations of paper clips
Red alligator clip		
Black alligator clip		

8. Examine the data you collected above.

Discussion:

1. Which paper clip had the most bubbles? _____

2. Explain why that paper clip had the most bubbles.

   _____

   _____

   _____

3. Which battery terminal produces the hydrogen gas? Explain why you think so.

   _____

   _____

   _____

4. Which terminal produces the oxygen gas? Explain why you think so.

   _____

   _____

Challenge:
Redesign this electrolysis apparatus to capture the hydrogen and oxygen.

Name: _____ Date: _____

Chapter Seven: Hydrogen Fuel Cells

Student Activity

Activity Three: Fuel Cell Car

Challenge Question: How does a fuel cell car work?

Materials:

      Fuel cell car kit   Masking tape   Meter sticks

TEACHER NOTE: This activity MUST be closely supervised by an adult.

Safety Precautions:
Read and follow all instructions.
Wear goggles.
Be trained by your teacher in the operation of the fuel cell.
Remove anything that could ignite the gases from the fuel cell.
Keep away from all flammable fuels.

Emergency Shut Down:
In the event that the hydrogen leaks, disconnect the electric cable from the fuel cell.
Initiate all necessary fire-fighting measures.
Make sure everyone stays at least 10 m away from the apparatus.
After 10 minutes, close down the apparatus.

Fuel Cell Safety:
Use in a well ventilated room.
Fill the fuel cell with distilled water only.
The hydrogen and oxygen reacting in the fuel cell cause a source of danger.
Do not operate the fuel cell without oxygen.
Only operate the fuel cell at room temperature.
Do not modify the fuel cell.
Only use the gas storage units provided.

Electrical Safety:
Shorted batteries can get very hot.
Do not dispose of batteries in a fire.
Electrolyte in the batteries is corrosive and can cause damage to eyes and skin.

Mechanical Safety:
Handle small parts and sharp wires carefully.
The gearbox contains small parts that may be a hazard to small children.
Keep fingers out of the moving parts of the car.

Name: _____   Date: _____

Chapter Seven: Hydrogen Fuel Cells

Student Activity

Procedure:

This activity MUST be closely supervised by an adult.

Do this activity in a well-ventilated area away from any gas or flames.

1. Construct the fuel cell car using the instructions provided by the manufacturer. Follow all instructions from the manufacturer.
2. Use masking tape to mark out at least a three-meter-long track for the car. This may have to be adjusted for your car.
3. Test the car on the track, and record your observations in the data table below.

Trial	Distance (m)	Observations
1		

4. Make any necessary adjustments that need to be made to make your car run better.

5. Record what you did to improve the car.

_____

_____

_____

_____

_____

6. Retest the car.
7. Record your observations in the data table below.

Trial	Distance (m)	Observations
2		

8. Find the average distance traveled for trial one and two. _____

9. What is the average distance the car can travel on one tank of hydrogen? _____

Name: _____   Date: _____

Chapter Seven: Hydrogen Fuel Cells

Student Activity

Discussion:

1. How was the hydrogen produced for the fuel cell?

    _____

    _____

    _____

    _____

    _____

2. Explain how the fuel cell works.

    _____

    _____

    _____

    _____

    _____

    _____

    _____

    _____

3. Draw a diagram of your fuel cell car. Label all of the parts.

Name: _____   Date: _____

Chapter Seven: Hydrogen Fuel Cells

Student Activity

4. Use the diagram to describe how the hydrogen gas was used to propel the car.

    _____

    _____

    _____

    _____

    _____

    _____

    _____

    _____

5. Describe the process used to produce the hydrogen and oxygen gas in the fuel cell.

    _____

    _____

    _____

    _____

    _____

    _____

    _____

    _____

Challenge:

1. Design a real car that could use hydrogen as its fuel source.
2. Design a car that would use hydrogen as its fuel source and that never has to be refueled.

Chapter Seven: Hydrogen Fuel Cells

Further Investigation: Hydrogen/Hydrogen Fuel Cells

Websites

A World In Motion: Fuel Cell Challenge
http://www.awim.org/curriculum/fuelcell/

Fuel Economy: Fuel Cell Vehicles
http://www.fueleconomy.gov/feg/fuelcell.shtml

Honda: Honda Begins Operations of New Solar Hydrogen Station
http://world.honda.com/news/2010/c100127 New-Solar-Hydrogen-Station/

Horizon Fuel Cell Technology Kits
http://www.horizonfuelcell.com/fuel_cell_stacks.htm

How Stuff Works: How Fuel Cells Work
http://auto.howstuffworks.com/fuel-efficiency/alternative-fuels/fuel-cell.htm

NEED Hydrogen
http://www.need.org/needpdf/infobook_activities/IntInfo/HydrogenI.pdf

National Renewable Energy Laboratory: Hydrogen & Fuel Cells Research
http://www.nrel.gov/hydrogen/

Renewable Energy World: Hydrogen Energy
http://www.renewableenergyworld.com/rea/tech/hydrogen

U.S. Department of Energy: Energy Efficiency & Renewable Energy: Fuel Cell Technologies Program
http://www1.eere.energy.gov/hydrogenandfuelcells/education/

U.S. Department of Energy: Hydrogen Program: Hydrogen Fuel Cells
http://www.hydrogen.energy.gov/pdfs/doe_fuelcellfactsheet.pdf

U.S. Energy Information Administration: Energy Kids: Hydrogen
http://tonto.eia.doe.gov/kids/energy.cfm?page=hydrogen_home-basics

Name: _____   Date: _____

Chapter Seven: Hydrogen Fuel Cells

Hydrogen Fuel Assessment

Objectives:
Students will be able to…
- Identify the forces that affect the movement of a car and how these forces can be overcome.
- Explain how a car works.
- Explain the function of the chassis, wheel and axle, engine, fuel, etc.
- Identify a problem; create a solution for the problem; construct, test, evaluate, and redesign the model as needed; identify the constraints and trade-offs made in using hydrogen as an energy source, and communicate the results.

Matching:

_____ 1.   Electrolysis

_____ 2.   Fuel cell

_____ 3.   Force

_____ 4.   Friction

_____ 5.   Drag

_____ 6.   Force of gravity

_____ 7.   Inertia

_____ 8.   Mass

a.   A push or pull on an object

b.   Use of electricity to produce a chemical change to break down water into hydrogen and oxygen

c.   Device that continuously changes a fuel's chemical energy into electrical energy.

d.   Tendency of objects to resist changes in motion

e.   Amount of matter present

f.   Force that resists motion

g.   Air resistance that slows a vehicle down

h.   Attraction that a planet has for objects near it

9.   Explain how hydrogen can be produced by the process of electrolysis.

_____

_____

_____

_____

_____

_____

Name: _____ Date: _____

10. Explain how a fuel cell works.

_____

_____

_____

_____

_____

11. Describe how the design of the car chassis impacts the fuel efficiency, speed, and purpose for the car.

_____

_____

_____

_____

_____

Assessment of Technological Design:

Directions: Fill in the chart with information about the fuel cell model car you made.

Technological Design	Indicator	Evidence
Identified the problem	Problem was identified	
Identified a possible solution for the problem	List of brainstorming solutions was provided and one solution was identified to test	
Constructed a model and plan for the solution	Plan states specifically what materials to be used and steps explaining how the materials will be used	
Tested the model and plan	Plan and model were tested, data was recorded	
Evaluated the model/plan	Results of the data were analyzed and the plan/model was evaluated, problems with the plan were identified, solutions to the problems were identified	
Redesigned the model/plan	Plan was redesigned to solve the identified problems in the first plan/model, and the new plan was tested and evaluated	
Identified constraints and trade-offs	3 constraints/trade-offs were described, and reasoning for trade-offs was explained	
Communicated the results	Presented plans and results to other students	

Chapter Eight: STEM Design Challenge

Teacher Information

Topic: Alternative Energy – Design a windmill that can be used to lift a small object.

Standards:
NSES – Unifying Concepts and Processes
Evidence, Models, and Explanations
Form and Function

NSES – Content
NSES A: Science as Inquiry
NSES B: Physical Science
NSES E: Science and Technology

NCTM:
Problem Solving
Communication
Reasoning
Statistics - Data collection and analysis
Measurement
Geometry

ITEA:
Nature of Technology
Technology and Society
Understanding and Abilities in Engineering Design

Concepts:
Alternative energy
Innovation
Wind energy
Renewable energy sources

Objectives:
Students will be able to…
• Identify a problem.
• Brainstorm solutions for the problem.
• Select the best solution to the problem.
• Construct a model.
• Test the model.
• Evaluate the model.
• Redesign the model.
• Test the redesigned model.
• Evaluate the redesigned model.
• Identify constraints/trade-offs.
• Communicate the results.

Activity: Student Design (p. 95)
Materials:
       A variety of recycled materials
       An electric fan

Chapter Eight: STEM Design Challenge

Student Information

Topic: Alternative Energy – Design a windmill that can be used to lift a small object.

Concepts:
Alternative energy
Innovation
Wind energy
Renewable energy sources

Objectives:
Students will be able to…
- Identify a problem.
- Brainstorm solutions for the problem.
- Select the best solution to the problem.
- Construct a model.
- Test the model.
- Evaluate the model.
- Redesign the model.
- Test the redesigned model.
- Evaluate the redesigned model.
- Identify constraints/trade-offs.
- Communicate the results.

STEM Challenge: Design and build a working windmill out of everyday products. The windmill, when placed 60 cm away from an electric fan set on high speed, must be able to rotate and lift a small object.

Content Background:

The Story of William Kamkwamba

William Kamkwamba lived in a small village in Malawi, Africa. He lived without running water or electricity to provide light, heating, and cooling. In 2002, there was a severe drought and famine in his village, so at age 14, he had to drop out of school because his family could not afford the $80 a year tuition.

Kamkwamba was fascinated by electricity. He found a book in the library that had a picture of a windmill and decided to try to help his family to get electricity and water by constructing the windmill he saw in the picture. There were no directions in the book. He just wanted to solve the problem of his parents not being able to afford electricity.

So he looked at the picture and some science textbooks and came up with a design plan. He could not afford to buy the materials needed, so he found scrap metal, tractor and bicycle parts, and blue-gum trees to construct a working windmill. Kamkwamba's first wind generator was built with recycled materials—a shoe, blades, a pole, some wires, and a small motor out of a cassette recorder. It produced enough electricity to power a small radio.

For three years, William worked on building, testing, designing, and redesigning his model. His large windmill powered four light bulbs with homemade switches and a circuit breaker in his family home. He constructed a second machine that powered a water pump to bring water into his village.

William Kamkwamba's first windmill

Chapter Eight: STEM Design Challenge

Student Information

Fourteen-year-old William Kamkwamba had a desire to solve a problem for his family. Through the use of science, technology, engineering, and mathematics, he solved the problem. His story did not end there. His story started a project called Moving Windmills. The Moving Windmills Project helps Malawian-run rural economic development and education projects in William's hometown in Malawi. The goals of this project included community economic independence and sustainability; food, water, and health security; and education.

For more information on William Kamkwamba's story, read: *The Boy Who Harnessed the Wind: Creating Currents of Electricity and Hope* by William Kamkwamba and Brian Mealer, Harper Collins Publishing.

Your challenge for this activity is to apply what you have learned about alternative energy sources to solve a problem. The steps you will be using are (1) identify a problem, (2) brainstorm ideas about how you might solve the problem, (3) draw a diagram of your model, (4) construct a model of your solution, (5) test your solution, (6) evaluate your solution, (7) identify how to improve your design, (8) make the needed changes, (9) retest and reevaluate your design, and (10) share your results.

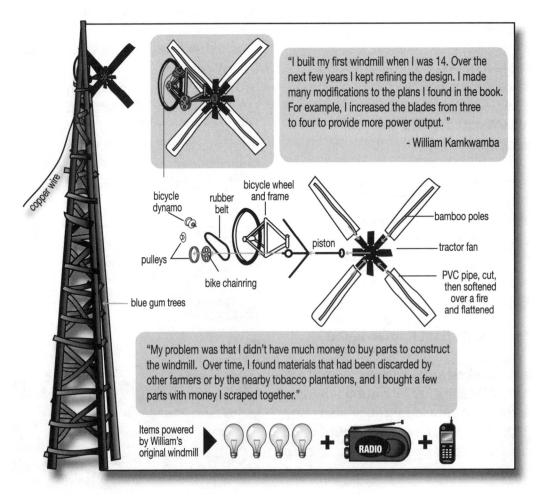

"I built my first windmill when I was 14. Over the next few years I kept refining the design. I made many modifications to the plans I found in the book. For example, I increased the blades from three to four to provide more power output."

- William Kamkwamba

bicycle dynamo
rubber belt
bicycle wheel and frame
copper wire
pulleys
bike chainring
blue gum trees
piston
bamboo poles
tractor fan
PVC pipe, cut, then softened over a fire and flattened

"My problem was that I didn't have much money to buy parts to construct the windmill. Over time, I found materials that had been discarded by other farmers or by the nearby tobacco plantations, and I bought a few parts with money I scraped together."

Items powered by William's original windmill ▶   + RADIO +

Moving Windmills, William's Story http://movingwindmills.org/story

Name: _____   Date: _____

Chapter Eight: STEM Design Challenge

Student Activity

Activity: Student Design

Materials:
  A variety of recycled materials

STEM Challenge Problem: Wind is a renewable alternative energy source that can be used to generate or supplement energy for homes and businesses. Design and build a working windmill out of everyday products. The windmill must be placed 60 cm away from an electric fan set on high speed. The blades of the windmill must be able to rotate, causing a small object to be lifted upward.

Procedure:

1. Identify the problem stated in the STEM Challenge Problem.

    _____

2. Brainstorm how you might solve the problem and record your ideas.

    _____

    _____

    _____

    _____

3. Identify one idea to test. _____

    _____

4. Design a model of the technology that will solve the problem. Draw a diagram of your model.

Name: _____   Date: _____

Chapter Eight: STEM Design Challenge

Student Activity

5. Create a plan that states specifically what materials are needed and the steps explaining how the materials will be used.

    _____

    _____

    _____

    _____

    _____

    _____

    _____

6. Construct a model.
7. Test the model.
8. Record your observations in a data table.

9. Analyze the data you collected.

    _____

    _____

    _____

10. Evaluate the model. Did the model work? Explain.

    _____

    _____

Name: _____   Date: _____

Chapter Eight: STEM Design Challenge

Student Activity

11. Did the model work like you thought it would? If not, identify the problems and explain.

_____

_____

_____

_____

_____

_____

12. Identify solutions to improve your model.

_____

_____

_____

_____

_____

_____

13. Redesign the model and draw a diagram.

Name: _____   Date: _____

Chapter Eight: STEM Design Challenge

Student Activity

14.   Construct and test the redesigned model.
15.   Record your observations in a data table.

16.   Explain how effectively the design changes helped solve the problem.

        _____

        _____

        _____

        _____

17.   Is there something else that could be done to improve the design? Explain.

        _____

        _____

        _____

        _____

18.   Identify and describe at least three constraints/trade-offs encountered when designing the wind-mill and explain the reason for the trade-offs.

        _____

        _____

        _____

        _____

19.   Communicate the results.

Chapter Eight: STEM Design Challenge

Further Investigation: Inventions, Innovation, Technology

A Science Odyssey
http://www.pbs.org/wgbh/aso/

Amazing Kids
http://www.amazing-kids.org/kids3-00.htm

American Inventors and Inventions
http://www.150.si.edu/150trav/remember/
amerinv.htm

Canada Science and Technology Museum
http://www.sciencetech.technomuses.ca/english/
schoolzone/invention/gallery.cfm

Engineer Girl
http://www.engineergirl.org/

Engineering Challenges
http://www.engineeringchallenges.org/

Engineering K-12
http://egfi-k12.org/

Engineering, Science, and Mathematics Careers
http://www.khake.com/page53.html

Engineer Your Life
http://www.engineeryourlife.org/

Fact Monster: A Guide to Inventions A-Z
http://www.factmonster.com/ipka/A0004637.html

Famous Inventions A-Z
http://inventors.about.com/od/astartinventions/a/
FamousInvention.htm

Girl Scouts: Girls Go Tech
http://www.girlsgotech.org/engineer.html

Greatest Engineering Achievements of the 20th Century
http://www.greatachievements.org/

How Stuff Works Express
http://express.howstuffworks.com/

Inventions and Technology
http://kids.nypl.org/science/inventions.cfm

Inventions, Inventors, and You
http://www.ih.k12.oh.us/MSHERRMANN/Invent2.
htm

Inventors and Inventions
http://edtech.kennesaw.edu/web/inventor.html

Kids and Energy - Energy Smart Inventions
http://www.kids.esdb.bg/smart_inventions.html

Kid Inventions: Inventions for School
http://inventors.about.com/od/kidinventions/ss/
Young_Inventors.htm

Kids Konnect: Inventors and Inventions
http://www.kidskonnect.com/subject-index/15-
science/86-inventors-a-inventions.html

Lemelson Center for the Study of Invention and Innovation
http://invention.smithsonian.org/resources/sites_
teachers.aspx

Moving Windmills
http://movingwindmills.org/

National Academy of Engineers
http://www.nae.edu

National Geographic: Green Car Puzzler
http://kids.nationalgeographic.com/kids/games/
puzzlesquizzes/green-cars-puzzler/

National Museum of Education: Invention
http://nmoe.org/students/index.htm

New York Public Library On-Lion: Inventions Changed Our World
http://teacher.scholastic.com/lessonrepro/lesson
plans/theme/inventions.htm

PBS: Forgotten Inventors
http://www.pbs.org/wgbh/amex/telephone/
sfeature/index.html

Quiz Your Noodle National Geographic Kids.
http://kids.nationalgeographic.com/kids/games/
puzzlesquizzes/quizyournoodle-revolutionary-
inventions/

Science Learning: Ben Franklin
http://sln.fi.edu/franklin/inventor/inventor.html

Smithsonian: Innovative Lives
http://invention.smithsonian.org/centerpieces/
ilives/

Spotlight: Biography Inventors
http://www.smithsonianeducation.org/spotlight/
inventors1.html

Name: _____   Date: _____

Chapter Eight: STEM Design Challenge

Design Challenge Assessment

Objectives:

Students will be able to…

- Identify a problem.
- Brainstorm solutions for the problem.
- Select the best solution to the problem.
- Construct a model.
- Test the model.
- Evaluate the model.
- Redesign the model.
- Test the redesigned model.
- Evaluate the redesigned model.
- Identify constraints/trade-offs.
- Communicate the results.

Assessment of Technological Design:

Directions: Fill in the chart with information about the models you made.

Technological Design	Indicator	Evidence
Identified the problem	Problem was identified	
Identified a possible solution for the problem	List of brainstorming solutions was provided and one solution was identified to test	
Constructed a model and plan for the solution	Plan states specifically what materials to be used and steps explaining how the materials will be used	
Tested the model and plan	Plan and model were tested, data was recorded	
Evaluated the model/plan	Results of the data were analyzed and the plan/model was evaluated, problems with the plan were identified, solutions to the problems were identified	
Redesigned the model/plan	Plan was redesigned to solve the identified problems in the first plan/model, and the new plan was tested and evaluated	
Identified constraints and trade-offs	3 constraints/trade-offs were described, and reasoning for trade-offs was explained	
Communicated the results	Presented plans and results to other students	

Name: _____ Date: _____

Science Inquiry Skills Assessment

Basic Skills	Indicators	Evidence that students demonstrated process skill
Classifying	Grouping, ordering, arranging, or distributing objects, events, or information into categories based on properties or criteria, according to some method or system.	
Observing	Using the senses (or extensions of the senses) to gather information about an object or event.	
Measuring	Using both standard and nonstandard measures or estimates to describe the dimensions of an object or event. Making quantitative observations.	
Inferring	Making an interpretation or conclusion based on reasoning to explain an observation.	
Communicating	Communicating ideas through speaking or writing. Students may share the results of investigations, collaborate on solving problems, and gather and interpret data both orally and in writing. Use graphs, charts, and diagrams to describe data.	
Predicting	Making a forecast of future events or conditions in the context of previous observations and experiences.	
Manipulating Materials	Handling or treating materials and equipment skillfully and effectively.	
Replicating	Performing acts that duplicate demonstrated symbols, patterns, or procedures.	
Using Numbers	Applying mathematical rules or formulas to calculate quantities or determine relationships from basic measurements.	
Developing Vocabulary	Specialized terminology and unique uses of common words in relation to a given topic need to be identified and given meaning.	
Questioning	Questions serve to focus inquiry, determine prior knowledge, and establish purposes or expectations for an investigation. An active search for information is promoted when questions are used.	
Using Cues	Key words and symbols convey significant meaning in messages. Organizational patterns facilitate comprehension of major ideas. Graphic features clarify textual information.	

Name: _____   Date: _____

Science Inquiry Skills Assessment

Integrated Skills	Indicators	Evidence that students demonstrated process skill
Creating Models	Displaying information by means of graphic illustrations or other multisensory representations.	
Formulating Hypotheses	Stating or constructing a statement that is testable about what is thought to be the expected outcome of an experiment (based on reasoning).	
Generalizing	Drawing general conclusions from particulars.	
Identifying & Controlling Variables	Recognizing the characteristics of objects or factors in events that are constant or change under different conditions and that can affect an experimental outcome, keeping most variables constant while manipulating only one (the independent) variable.	
Defining Operationally	Stating how to measure a variable in an experiment; defining a variable according to the actions or operations to be performed on or with it.	
Recording & Interpreting Data	Collecting bits of information about objects and events that illustrate a specific situation, organizing and analyzing data that have been obtained, and drawing conclusions from it by determining apparent patterns or relationships in the data.	
Making Decisions	Identifying alternatives and choosing a course of action from among alternatives after basing the judgment for the selection on justifiable reasons.	
Experimenting	Being able to conduct an experiment, including asking an appropriate question, stating a hypothesis, identifying and controlling variables, operationally defining those variables, designing a "fair" experiment, and interpreting the results of an experiment.	

Science Process Skills

	Skills	Definition
B A S I C **P R O C E S S** **S K I L L S**	Classifying	Grouping, ordering, arranging, or distributing objects, events, or information into categories based on properties or criteria, according to some method or system.
	Observing	Using the senses (or extensions of the senses) to gather information about an object or event.
	Measuring	Using both standard and nonstandard measures or estimates to describe the dimensions of an object or event. Making quantitative observations.
	Inferring	Making an interpretation or conclusion based on reasoning to explain an observation.
	Communicating	Communicating ideas through speaking or writing. Students may share the results of investigations, collaborate on solving problems, and gather and interpret data both orally and in writing. Use graphs, charts, and diagrams to describe data.
	Predicting	Making a forecast of future events or conditions in the context of previous observations and experiences.
	Manipulating Materials	Handling or treating materials and equipment skillfully and effectively.
	Replicating	Performing acts that duplicate demonstrated symbols, patterns, or procedures.
	Using Numbers	Applying mathematical rules or formulas to calculate quantities or determine relationships from basic measurements.
	Developing Vocabulary	Specialized terminology and unique uses of common words in relation to a given topic need to be identified and given meaning.
	Questioning	Questions serve to focus inquiry, determine prior knowledge, and establish purposes or expectations for an investigation. An active search for information is promoted when questions are used.
	Using Cues	Key words and symbols convey significant meaning in messages. Organizational patterns facilitate comprehension of major ideas. Graphic features clarify textual information.

	Skills	Definition
I N T E G R A T E D **S K I L L S**	Creating Models	Displaying information by means of graphic illustrations or other multisensory representations.
	Formulating Hypotheses	Stating or constructing a statement that is testable about what is thought to be the expected outcome of an experiment (based on reasoning).
	Generalizing	Drawing general conclusions from particulars.
	Identifying & Controlling Variables	Recognizing the characteristics of objects or factors in events that are constant or change under different conditions and that can affect an experimental outcome, keeping most variables constant while manipulating only one (the independent) variable.
	Defining Operationally	Stating how to measure a variable in an experiment; defining a variable according to the actions or operations to be performed on or with it.
	Recording & Interpreting Data	Collecting bits of information about objects and events that illustrate a specific situation, organizing and analyzing data that have been obtained, and drawing conclusions from it by determining apparent patterns or relationships in the data.
	Making Decisions	Identifying alternatives and choosing a course of action from among alternatives after basing the judgment for the selection on justifiable reasons.
	Experimenting	Being able to conduct an experiment, including asking an appropriate question, stating a hypothesis, identifying and controlling variables, operationally defining those variables, designing a "fair" experiment, and interpreting the results of an experiment.

NSES Content Standards

Summary from the NRC (1996). *National Science Education Standards.* Washington, D.C.: National Academy Press.

Assumptions:
1. NSES Standards require changes throughout the system.
2. What students learn is influenced by how they are taught.
3. Actions of teachers are deeply influenced by their perceptions of science as an enterprise and as a subject to be taught and learned.
4. Student understanding is actively constructed through individual and social processes.
5. Actions of teachers are deeply influenced by their understanding of and relationships with students.

NSES Unifying Concepts and Processes:
Systems, order, and organization
Evidence, models, and explanations
Change, constancy, and measurement
Evolution and equilibrium
Form and function

NSES Content Standards:

Standard	Understanding	Indicators Grades 5–8 Students will be able to:
A. Science as Inquiry	Abilities to do scientific inquiry	Identify questions that can be answered through investigations.
		Plan and conduct a scientific investigation.
		Use appropriate tools and techniques to gather, analyze, and interpret data.
		Develop descriptions, explanations, predictions, and models using evidence.
		Think critically and logically to make the relationships between evidence and explanations.
		Recognize and analyze alternative explanations and predictions.
		Communicate scientific procedures and explanations.
		Use mathematics in all aspects of inquiry.
	Understanding scientific inquiry	Explain that different kinds of investigations are needed depending on the questions they are trying to answer.
		Explain that current scientific knowledge guides scientific investigations.
		Explain that mathematics is important to all aspects of inquiry.
		Explain that technology used to gather data increases accuracy and quantifies the results.
		Explain that scientists develop explanations from evidence from investigations and scientific knowledge.
		Explain that science advances through skepticism.
		Explain that scientific investigations may result in new ideas and investigations.

B. Physical Science	Properties and changes in properties of matter	Explain that substances have characteristic properties.
		Explain that substances react chemically in characteristic ways with other substances to form new substances (compounds) with different properties. Mass is conserved in chemical reactions.
		Explain that chemical elements do not break down during normal laboratory reactions. There are over 100 known elements that combine to form compounds.
	Motions and Forces	Explain that motion can be described by its position, speed, and direction and can be measured.
		Explain an object in motion will move at a constant speed in a straight line until acted upon by another force.
		Explain if more than one force acts upon an object along a straight line, the forces either reinforce or cancel one another. Unbalanced forces will cause changes in the speed or direction of the motion.
	Transfer of Energy	Explain that energy is a property of many substances and is transferred in many ways.
		Explain that heat moves in predictable ways, flowing from warmer to cooler areas until the temperature is equalized.
		Explain that light interacts with matter by transmission (including refraction), absorption, and scattering (including reflection).
		Explain electrical circuits are a means of transferring electrical energy.
		Explain that in most chemical and nuclear reactions energy is transferred into or out of a system.
		Explain that the sun is a major source of energy for changes on the earth's surface. The sun's energy arrives as light with a range of wavelengths—visible light, infrared, ultraviolet radiation.
C. Life Science	Structure and function of living systems	Explain that living systems demonstrate the complementary nature of function and structure. Levels of organization include cell, tissue, organ, systems, organism, and ecosystems.
		Explain that all organisms are composed of cells.
		Explain that cells carry on functions needed to sustain life, they grow and divide, take in nutrients, and get rid of wastes.
		Explain that specialized cells perform special functions. Groups of specialized cells make tissues; groups of specialized tissues form organs.
		Explain that humans have systems for digestion, respiration, reproduction, circulation, excretion, movement, control and coordination, and protection from diseases.
		Explain that disease is a breakdown in structures or functions of an organism.
	Reproduction and heredity	Explain that reproduction is a characteristic of all living systems.
		Explain in many species females produce eggs and males produce sperm. Egg and sperm unite to form a new organism. The new organism receives genetic information from the male and female.

		Explain that organisms require a set of instructions to specify its traits. Heredity is the passage of these instructions from one generation to another.
		Explain heredity information is contained in the genes in the chromosomes of each cell. A gene carries a single unit of information. Inherited traits are determined by the genes.
		Explain that characteristics of an organism are from the combination of traits. Some traits are inherited and some are from interactions with the environment.
	Regulation and behavior	Explain that all organisms must be able to obtain and use resources, grow, reproduce, and maintain stable internal conditions in a constantly changing environment.
		Explain that regulation of the internal environment involves sensing the environment and changing physiological activities to keep conditions within the range required to survive.
		Explain that behavior is one kind of response an organism makes to an internal or external stimulus.
		Explain that an organism's behavior evolves through adaptation to its environment.
	Populations and ecosystems	Describe a population as all individuals of a species that occur at a given place in a given time. An ecosystem is all populations and the physical factors with which they interact.
		Explain that populations can be categorized by the function they serve in an ecosystem—producers, consumers, decomposers. Food webs identify the relationships among organisms.
		Explain that the major source of energy in an ecosystem is sunlight.
		Explain that the number of organisms in an ecosystem depends on the resources available and abiotic factors.
	Diversity and adaptations of organisms	Explain that millions of species are alive today.
		Explain that biological evolution accounts for the diversity of species.
		Explain that extinction of a species occurs when an environment changes and it cannot adapt.
D. Earth Science	Structure of the earth system	Describe that the earth is layered with a lithosphere (crust), hot convecting mantle, and dense metal core.
		Explain that lithospheric (crustal) plates constantly move in response to movements in the mantle.
		Explain that landforms result from constructive and destructive forces.
		Describe the rock cycle as some of the changes in the solid earth.
		Describe soil as weathered rocks and decomposed organic matter.
		Explain that water covers the majority of the earth and it circulates through the crust, water, and atmosphere (water cycle).
		Explain that water is a solvent and dissolves minerals and gases as it passes through the water cycle.

		Explain that the atmosphere is a mixture of nitrogen, oxygen, and trace gases.
		Explain that clouds are formed by condensation.
		Explain that global patterns of atmospheric movement influence local weather.
		Explain that living organisms play many roles in the earth system.
	Earth's history	Explain that earth processes—erosion, movement of plates, and changes in the atmosphere—also occurred in the past.
		Explain that fossils provide evidence of the past.
	Earth in the solar system	Explain that the earth is the third planet from the sun in the solar system. The sun is an average star and is the central and largest body in the solar system.
		Explain most objects in the solar system are in regular predictable motion.
		Explain that gravity is the force that keeps planets in orbit around the sun. It holds everything on earth and controls the tides.
		Explain that the sun is the major source of energy for phenomena on the earth's surface.
E. Science and Technology	Abilities of technological design	Identify appropriate problems for technological design.
		Design a solution or product.
		Implement a proposed design.
		Evaluate completed designs or products.
		Communicate the process of technological design.
	Understanding of technological design	Explain that scientists propose explanations for the natural world. Engineers propose solutions relating to human needs, problems, and aspirations. Technological solutions are temporary; exist within nature so they can not contravene physical or biological principles; solutions may have side effects and costs, carry risks, and provide benefits.
		Explain many different people from many cultures have contributed to science and technology.
		Explain that science drives technology, and technology is essential to science.
		Explain that designed solutions are not perfect; they have trade-offs and risks.
		Explain that technological designs have constraints.
		Explain that technological solutions have intended benefits and unintended consequences.
F. Personal and Social Perspectives	Personal health	Regular exercise is important to maintain and improve health.
		Potential for accidents and hazards create a need for injury prevention.
		Use of tobacco increases the risk of illness.
		Alcohol and other drugs are often abused substances.
		Food provides energy and nutrients for growth and development.
		Sex drive is a natural human function that needs understanding.

		Natural environments may contain substances that are harmful to human beings.
	Populations, resources, and environments	Overpopulated environments will become degraded due to increased use of resources.
		Causes of environmental degradation and resources vary.
	Natural hazards	Internal and external processes of the earth cause natural hazards.
		Human activities can also cause natural hazards.
		Natural hazards can present personal and societal changes.
	Risks and benefits	Risk analysis considers the type of hazard and estimates the number of people that might be exposed and the number likely to suffer consequences.
		Risks are associated with natural hazards, chemical hazards, biological hazards, social hazards, and personal hazards.
		A systematic approach should be used for risk benefit analysis.
		Personal and social decisions are made based on perceptions of risks and benefits.
	Science and technology in society	Science influences society through its knowledge and world view.
		Societal challenges often inspire questions for scientific research and social priorities influence research through availability of funding.
		Technology influences society through its products and processes.
		Science and technology have advanced through different people in different cultures in different times in history.
		Scientists and engineers work in different settings.
		Scientists and engineers have ethical codes.
		Science cannot answer all questions and technology cannot solve all problems.
G. History and Nature of Science	Science as a human endeavor	People of diverse backgrounds engage in science, engineering, and related fields.
		Science requires different abilities.
	The nature of science	Scientists formulate and test explanations using observations, experiments, and theoretical and mathematic models.
		Scientists may have different opinions.
		Scientific inquiry includes evaluating results of investigations, experiments, observations, theoretical models, and explanations of other scientists.
	The history of science	Many individuals have contributed to the traditions of science.
		Science has been practiced by different individuals in different cultures.
		History shows how difficult it was for scientific innovators to break through the accepted ideas of their times.

Principles and Standards for School Mathematics 5–8 (NCTM)

National Council for Teachers of Mathematics. (2000). *Principles and Standards for School Mathematics*. Reston, VA: National Council for Teachers of Mathematics.

Standard	Indicators
Problem Solving	Use problem-solving approaches to investigate and understand mathematics.
	Formulate problems from situations.
	Develop and apply a variety of strategies to solve problems.
	Verify and interpret results.
	Generalize solutions and strategies to new problems.
	Acquire confidence in using mathematics.
Communication	Model situations using oral, written, concrete, pictorial, graphical, and algebraic methods.
	Reflect on and clarify their own thinking about mathematical ideas and situations.
	Develop common understandings of mathematical ideas.
	Use the skills of reading, listening, and viewing to interpret and evaluate mathematical ideas.
	Discuss mathematical ideas and make conjectures and arguments.
	Appreciate the value of mathematical notation.
Reasoning	Recognize and apply deductive and inductive reasoning.
	Use reasoning processes.
	Make and evaluate conjectures and arguments.
	Validate their own thinking.
	Appreciate the pervasive use and power of reasoning as a part of mathematics.
Mathematical Connections	See mathematics as an integrated whole.
	Explore problems and describe results using graphs; numbers; and physical, algebraic, and verbal models or representations.
	Use a mathematical idea to further their understanding of mathematics.
	Apply mathematical thinking and modeling to solve problems.
	Value the role of mathematics in our culture and society.
Number and Number Relationships	Use numbers in a variety of forms.
	Develop number sense.
	Use ratios, proportions, and percents in a variety of situations.
	Investigate relationships among fractions, decimals, and percents.
	Represent numerical relationships on graphs.
Number Systems/ Number Theory	Understand the need for numbers beyond whole numbers.
	Develop and use order relations.
	Extend understanding of whole number operations to fractions, decimals, integers, and rational numbers.
	Understand how basic arithmetic operations are related to one another.
	Develop and apply number theory in real-world problems.
Computation and Estimation	Compute with whole numbers, fractions, decimals, integers, and rational numbers.
	Develop, analyze, and explain methods for computation and estimation.
	Select and use appropriate methods for computing.
	Use computation, estimation, and proportions to solve problems.
	Use estimation to check reasonableness.

Patterns and Functions	Describe, extend, analyze, and create patterns.
	Describe and represent relationships with tables, graphs, and rules.
	Analyze functional relationships to explain how a change in one changes another.
	Use patterns and functions to represent and solve problems.
Algebra	Understand variables, expressions, and equations.
	Represent situations and number patterns with tables, graphs, verbal rules, and equations and their interrelationships.
	Analyze tables and graphs to identify properties and relationships.
	Develop confidence in solving linear equations.
	Investigate inequalities and nonlinear equations.
	Apply algebraic methods to solve problems.
Statistics	Systematically collect, organize, and describe data.
	Construct, read, and interpret tables, graphs, and charts.
	Make inferences and arguments based on data analysis.
	Evaluate arguments based on data analysis.
	Develop appreciation for statistical methods for decision making.
Probability	Model situations by devising and carrying out experiments or simulations to determine probabilities.
	Model situations by constructing a sample space to determine probabilities.
	Appreciate the power of using a probability model.
	Make predictions based on experimental or theoretical probabilities.
	Develop an appreciation for the use of probability in the real world.
Geometry	Identify, describe, compare, and classify geometric figures.
	Visualize and represent geometric figures.
	Explore transformations of geometric figures.
	Represent and solve problems using geometric figures.
	Understand and apply geometric properties and relationships.
	Develop appreciation of geometry as a means of describing the physical world.
Measurement	Extend understanding of processes of measurement.
	Estimate, make, and use measurement to describe and compare phenomena.
	Select appropriate units and tools.
	Understand the structure and use of measurement systems.
	Understand perimeter, area, volume, angle measurement, capacity, weight, and mass.
	Develop concepts of rate and other derived and indirect measurements.
	Develop formulas and procedures for determining measures to solve problems.

ITEA Standards for Technological Literacy

Adapted from: International Technology Education Association (2007) *Standards for technological literacy*. Reston, VA: International Technology Education Association. URL: www.iteaconnect.org

Standards for Technological Literacy:

Goal	Standard	Grades 6–8 Indicators
Students will develop an understanding of the Nature of Technology.	Students will develop understanding of:	Students will be able to:
	1. Characteristics and scope of technology	Explain that new products and systems can be developed to solve problems or help do things that could not be done without the help of technology.
		Explain that technology is a human activity and is the result of individual and collective needs and the ability to be creative.
		Explain that technology is closely linked to creativity which has resulted in innovation.
		Explain that corporations can create a demand for a product by bringing it onto a market and advertising it.
	2. Core concepts of technology	Describe that technological systems include input, processes, output, and feedback.
		Explain that technological systems can be connected to one another.
		Explain that malfunctions of any part of a system may affect the function and quality of the system.
		Describe that trade-off is a decision process recognizing the need for careful compromises among competing factors.
		Explain that different technologies involve different sets of processes.
		Describe maintenance as a process of inspecting and servicing a product or system on a regular basis so that it continues to function properly, to extend life or upgrade its capability.
		Describe that controls are mechanisms or particular steps performed using information about the system that causes systems to change.
	3. Relationships among technologies and the connections between technology and other fields	Explain that technological systems often interact with one another.
		Explain that a product, system, or environment developed for one setting may be applied to another setting.
		Explain that knowledge from other fields has a direct effect on the development of technology.
Students will develop an understanding of Technology and Society.	Students will develop understanding of:	Students will be able to:
	4. Cultural, social, economic, and political effects of technology	Explain that the use of technology affects humans in various ways—safety, comfort, choices, and attitudes about technology's development and use.

		Explain that technology is neither good nor bad, but the decisions about the use of it can result in desirable or undesirable consequences.
		Explain that development and use of technology poses ethical questions.
		Explain that economic, political, and cultural issues are influenced by the development and use of technology.
	5. Effects of technology on the environment	Explain the management of waste produced by technological systems is a societal issue.
		Explain that technologies can be used to repair damage caused by natural disasters and break down wastes.
		Explain that the development and use of technologies put environmental and economic concerns in competition with one another.
	6. Role of society in the development and use of technology	Explain that throughout history new technologies have resulted from demands, values, and interests of individuals, businesses, industries, and societies.
		Explain that the use of inventions and innovations has led to changes in society and creation of new needs and wants.
		Explain that social and cultural priorities and values are reflected in the technological devices.
		Explain that meeting social expectations is the driving force behind the acceptance and use of products and systems.
	7. The influence of technology on history	Explain that many inventions and innovations have evolved by using a methodical process of tests and refinements.
		Explain the specialization of function has been at the head of many technological improvements.
		Explain that the design and construction of structures for service or convenience have evolved from the development of techniques for measurement, controlling systems, and understanding of spatial relationships.
		Explain that in the past, an invention or innovation was not usually developed with the knowledge of science.
Students will develop an understanding of Design	Students will develop an understanding of:	Students will be able to:
	8. The attributes of design	Describe design as a creative process that leads to useful products and systems.
		Explain there is no perfect design.
		Explain that the requirements for a design are made up of criteria and constraints.
	9. Engineering design	Explain that design involves a set of steps that can be performed in different sequences and repeated as needed.
		Describe brainstorming—a group problem solving process in which each person presents their ideas in an open forum.
		Explain that modeling, testing, evaluating, and modifying are used to transform ideas into practical solutions.
	10. The role of troubleshooting, research and development, invention and innovation, and experimentation in problem solving	Describe troubleshooting as a way of identifying the cause of a malfunction in a technological system.
		Explain that invention is a process of turning ideas and imagination into devices and systems. Explain innovation is the process of modifying an existing product to improve it.

		Explain that some technological problems are best solved through science experimentations.
Students will develop Abilities for a Technological World.	Students will be able to:	Students will be able to:
	11. Apply the design process	Apply a design process to solve a problem.
		Make two- and three-dimensional representations of the design solution.
		Test and evaluate the design related to pre-established criteria.
		Make a product or system and document the solution.
	12. Use and maintain technological products and systems	Use information provided to see and understand how things work.
		Use tools, materials, and machines safely to diagnose, adjust, and repair systems.
		Use computers and calculators in various applications.
		Operate and maintain systems in order to achieve a given purpose.
	13. Assess the impact of products and systems	Design and use instruments to gather data.
		Use data collected to analyze and interpret trends in order to identify the positive or negative effects of a technology.
		Identify trends and monitor potential consequences of technological development.
		Interpret and evaluate the accuracy of the information obtained, and determine if it is useful.
Students will develop an understanding of the Designed World.	Students will develop an understanding of and be able to select and use the following:	Students will be able to:
	14. Medical technologies	Explain that advances in medical technologies are used to improve health care.
		Explain that sanitation processes used in the disposal of medical products help protect people from harmful organisms and disease and shape the ethics of medical safety.
		Explain that vaccines developed for immunizations require specialized technologies to support environments in which sufficient amounts of vaccines are produced.
		Describe that genetic engineering involves modifying the structure of DNA to produce novel genetic makeups.
	15. Agricultural and related biotechnologies	Explain that technological advances in agriculture affect the time and number of people required to produce food for large populations.
		Explain that a wide range of specialized equipment and practices are used to improve the production of food, fiber, fuel, and other products and in the care of animals.
		Describe that biotechnology applies the principles of biology to create products or processes.
		Explain that artificial ecosystems are human made environments that are designed to replicate a natural environment.
		Describe that the development of refrigeration, freezing, dehydration, preservation, and irradiation provide long-term storage of food and reduce the health risks of tainted food.

	16. Energy and power technologies	Explain that energy has the capacity to do work.
		Explain that energy can be used to do work using many processes.
		Explain that power is the rate at which energy is converted from one form to another, or transferred from one place to another, or the rate at which work is done.
		Describe that power systems are used to drive and provide propulsion to other products and systems.
		Explain that much of the energy used in our environment is not used efficiently.
	17. Information and communication technologies	Explain that information and communication allow information to be transferred from human to human, human to machine, and machine to human.
		Describe communication systems are made up of a source, encoder, transmitter, receiver, decoder, and destination.
		Describe that the design of a message is influenced by: intended audience, medium, purpose, and nature of the message.
		Explain the use of symbols, measurements, and drawings promotes clear communication by providing a common language to express ideas.
	18. Transportation technologies	Describe that transporting people and goods involves a combination of individuals or vehicles.
		Explain that transportation vehicles are made up of subsystems that must function together.
	19. Manufacturing technologies	Explain that manufacturing systems use mechanical processes that change the form of materials.
		Explain that manufactured goods can be durable or nondurable.
		Describe that the manufacturing process includes: designing, development, making, and servicing products and systems.
		Explain that chemical technologies are used to modify or alter chemical substances.
		Explain that materials must be located before they can be extracted from the earth.
		Explain that marketing involves informing the public about it as well as assisting in selling and distribution.
	20. Construction technologies	Explain that the selection of designs for structures is based on: building laws, codes, style, convenience, cost, climate, and function.
		Explain that structures rest on a foundation.
		Explain that some structures are temporary and some are permanent.
		Explain that buildings contain subsystems.

Assessment Answer Keys

Chapter One: Alternative Energy Assessment (p. 14–15)

1. b   2. d   3. a   4. g
5. e   6. c   7. h   8. f
9–11. Answers will vary.
12. Renewable energy sources can be restored in a short period of time. Examples of renewable energy sources are biomass, geothermal, solar, hydropower, and wind. Nonrenewable energy sources are limited. Examples of nonrenewable energy sources are coal, petroleum, natural gas, propane, and uranium.

Chapter Two: Oil Spill Assessment (p. 29–30)

1. Tanker collisions, off-shore drilling accidents, pipeline ruptures, etc.
2. Oil floats on water, amount of oil spilled, kind of oil spilled, amount of water affected, size of area covered, materials and resources available, cost, constraints and trade-offs, etc.
3. Costs, time, thoroughness
4. Oil spills coat the water and land with oil. This kills plants and animals. The oil may impact breeding or feeding areas. When the oil weathers, it releases toxic chemicals.
5. Animals get coated in oil and die of hypothermia. They ingest it, which affects their internal organs, or they breath in toxic fumes. Oil also impacts food chains.

Chapter Three: Compressed Air Assessment (p. 39–40)

1. Answers will vary.
2. The air rushing out under the craft provides a cushion of air under the craft that provides lift to the vehicle. The moving air propels it forward.
3. Newton's Law of Action and Reaction explains how the car works. The air rushes out of the balloon and pushes the car forward.
4. Compressed air is a renewable resource because it can be restored by adding more air.

Chapter Four: Wind Energy Assessment (p. 51–52)

1. The wind hits the sail and pushes the boat forward.
2. Wind can turn a wind turbine. The wind turbine turns a generator to make the electricity.
3. A wind turbine should be placed where there is wind that blows consistently.
4. Wind is a renewable resource because it can be restored by more wind. It does not run out.

Chapter Five: Solar Power Assessment (p. 66–67)

1. d   2. c   3. b   4. e   5. a
6. Answers will vary.
7. Photovoltaic cells absorb the radiant energy of the sun and convert it directly into electrical energy.
8. Solar collectors absorb radiant (solar) energy, convert it into heat, and store the heat (thermal energy).
9. Answers will vary.
10. Solar energy is a renewable resource because it can be restored with more energy from the sun.

Chapter Six: Biomass Assessment (p. 74–75)

1. a   2. c   3. b   4. d   5. e
6. Answers will vary.
7. Answers will vary.

Chapter Seven: Hydrogen Fuel Assessment (p. 90–91)

1. b   2. c   3. a   4. f
5. g   6. h   7. d   8. e
9–11. Answers will vary.

Chapter Eight: STEM Design Challenge Assessment (p. 100)

Answers will vary. Teacher check assessment rubric.

References

NOTE: Some of the activities in this book are from the Society of Automotive Engineers International (SAE) World in Motion curriculum materials. They are adapted to fit the parameters of this book. The full activities in the World in Motion curriculum materials demonstrate the whole engineering and technological design process. They were developed for grades K through college and beyond.

The SAE is a nonprofit scientific organization dedicated to the advancement of mobility technology. The SAE Foundation was organized in 1986 to promote and expand the engineering profession. The World in Motion Curriculum can be acquired from the Society of Automotive Engineers International.

The Kits include one classroom set of all of the materials needed. The teacher's materials include an overview of the vehicle, an introduction to the challenge, a description of the processes of engineering design, objectives for the activities, science skills, technology education, and correlations with the national science standards and benchmarks. It also includes the materials list, a calendar for the three weeks of the challenge, glossary, the content background for the investigation, and how the vehicle works and what difficulties the students might have in conducting the investigation.

The "Jet Toy" activity sets up a challenge that a toy company wants students to design a new line of balloon powered vehicles. In the "Skimmer" activity, the students are challenged to design a sail for a sailboat. The "Fuel Cell Car" curriculum leads students through how cars are designed, how a fuel cell works, and using the engineering design process to design a fuel cell car. The curriculum takes them through the steps of design engineering, starting with a challenge. Call for more information, 724-776-4841 or visit the World in Motion website: http://www.awim.org/curriculum/jettoy/

Articles

BBC News (May 21, 2010) "US Coast Guard Sets Fire to Oil Leaking in the Gulf."
http://news.bbc.co.uk/2/hi/americas/8649862.stm

Dillow, C. (2010) "System Stores Wind and Solar Power in the Form of Natural Gas, to Fit Neatly into Existing Infrastructure."
http://www.popsci.com/science/article/2010-05/carbon-neutral-natural-gas-made-wind-and-solar-could-power-existing-infrastructures

Hsu, J. (2009) "Scaly BMW Concept Car Collects Solar Power, Then Raises Panels to Brake."
http://www.popsci.com/cars/article/2009-10/bmw-concept-car-harnesses-solar-scale-air-brakes

Locke, S. (2009) "China Plans World's Largest Solar Power Plant."
http://www.popsci.com/scitech/article/2009-09/biggest-solar-power-plant-set-

The New York Times. (2009) "U.S. Solar Firm Cracks Chinese Market."
http://green.blogs.nytimes.com/2009/09/08/china-signs-deal-with-first-solar/

Olvera, Jennifer. (2008) "5 Things You Need to Know About Oil Dependency"
http://www.greencar.com/articles/5-things-need-oil-dependency.php

Olvera, Jennifer. (2008) "5 Things You Need to Know About Petroleum Violation Escrow Account"
http://www.greencar.com/articles/5-things-need-petroleum-violation-escrow-account.php

Roberts, D. (2009) "Solar Power: Harnessing the Terawatts of Energy We Get From the Sun."
http://www.popsci.com/environment/article/2009-06/solar-power

Sato, Shigeru, and Yugi Okada. (2009) "Mitsubishi, IHI to Join $21 Bln Space Solar Project (Update1)."
http://bloomberg.com/apps/news?pid=news archive&sid=aJ5291/

Websites

Amazing Kids
http://www.amazing-kids.org/kids3-00.htm

American Inventors and Inventions
http://www.150.si.edu/150trav/remember/amerinv.htm

A Science Odyssey
http://www.pbs.org/wgbh/aso/

A World In Motion: Fuel Cell Challenge
http://www.awim.org/curriculum/fuelcell/

Biomass Energy Resource Center
http://www.biomasscenter.org/

Biomass Magazine
http://www.biomassmagazine.com/

Biomass One: Renewable Energy
http://www.biomassone.com/

Biomass Power Association
http://www.usabiomass.org/

British Petroleum
http://www.bp.com/extendedsectiongeneric
article.do?categoryID=40&contentID=7061813

Canada Science and Technology Museum
http://www.sciencetech.technomuses.ca/english/schoolzone/invention/gallery.cfm

Chicago Museum of Science and Industry: Smart Home
http://www.msichicago.org/whats-here/exhibits/smart-home/

Department of the Interior
http://www.doi.gov

Discover Hover
http://www.discoverhover.org/

The Encyclopedia of Earth: *Exxon Valdez* Oil Spill
http://www.eoearth.org/article/Exxon_Valdez_oil_spill

Energy Justice Network Fact Sheet: Biomass Incineration
http://www.energyjustice.net/biomass/

Engineer Girl
http://www.engineergirl.org/

Engineering Challenges
http://www.engineeringchallenges.org/

Engineering K-12
http://egfi-k12.org/

Engineering, Science, and Mathematics Careers
http://www.khake.com/page53.html

Engineer Your Life
http://www.engineeryourlife.org/

Environmental Protection Agency
http://www.epa.gov/

Fact Monster: A Guide to Inventions A-Z
http://www.factmonster.com/ipka/A0004637.html

Famous Inventions A-Z
http://inventors.about.com/od/astartinventions/a/FamousInvention.htm

Fuel Economy: Fuel Cell Vehicles
http://www.fueleconomy.gov/feg/fuelcell.shtml

Future Cars: Human Car
http://www.futurecars.com/future-cars/electric-cars/earth-day-special-the-human-car-hc-imagineps

Girl Scouts: Girls Go Tech
http://www.girlsgotech.org/engineer.html

Gizmag.com: The Air Car
www.gizmag.com/go/7000/

Greatest Engineering Achievements of the 20th Century
http://www.greatachievements.org/

Green Jobs
http://www.greenjobs.com/Public/info/
industry_background.aspx?id=13

Honda: Honda Begins Operations of New Solar Hydrogen Station
http://world.honda.com/news/2010/c100127
New-Solar-Hydrogen-Station/

Horizon Fuel Cell Technology Kits
http://www.horizonfuelcell.com/

Hoverclub of America
http://www.hoverclubofamerica.org/

The Hovercraft Museum Trust
http://www.hovercraft-museum.org/museum.
html

How Stuff Works
http://science.howstuffworks.com

  How Stuff Works Express
  http://express.howstuffworks.com/

  How Stuff Works: How Fuel Cells Work
  http://auto.howstuffworks.com/fuel-
  efficiency/alternative-fuels/fuel-cell.htm

  How Stuff Works: How Solar Cells Work
  http://science.howstuffworks.com/
  solar-cell1.htm

  How Stuff Works: How Wind Power Works
  http://science.howstuffworks.com/
  wind-power7.htm

Intergovernmental Panel on Climate Change
http://www.ipcc.ch/

International Bird Rescue Research Center
http://www.ibrrc.org/

Inventions and Technology
http://kids.nypl.org/science/inventions.cfm

Inventions, Inventors, and You
http://www.ih.k12.oh.us/MSHERRMANN/
Invent2.htm

Inventors and Inventions
http://edtech.kennesaw.edu/web/inventor.html

Iowa Public Television: Explore More – The Future of Energy: Biomass
http://www.iptv.org/exploremore/energy/
profiles/biomass.cfm

Kids and Energy – Energy Smart Inventions
http://www.kids.esdb.bg/smart_inventions.html

Kid Inventions: Inventions for School
http://inventors.about.com/od/kidinventions/
ss/Young_Inventors.htm

Kids Konnect: Inventors and Inventions
http://www.kidskonnect.com/subject-index/
15-science/86-inventors-a-inventions.html

Kid Wind Project
http://www.kidwind.org/

Lemelson Center for the Study of Invention and Innovation
http://invention.smithsonian.org/resources/
sites_teachers.aspx

Marine Mammal Center, Sausalito, CA
http://www.marinemammalcenter.org/

Motor Development International
www.mdi.lu.english/

Moving Windmills
http://movingwindmills.org/

National Academy of Engineers
http://www.nae.edu

NASA: Life in a Greenhouse
http://spaceplace.jpl.nasa.gov/en/kids/tes/gases/

National Geographic Kids: Green Car Puzzler
http://kids.nationalgeographic.com/kids/games/puzzlesquizzes/green-cars-puzzler/

National Geographic Kids: Quiz Your Noodle
http://kids.nationalgeographic.com/kids/games/puzzlesquizzes/quizyournoodle-revolutionary-inventions/

National Museum of Education: Invention
http://nmoe.org/students/index.htm

National Energy Education Development (NEED) Project
http://www.need.org/

NEED Biomass
http://www.need.org/needpdf/infobook_activities/IntInfo/BiomassI.pdf

NEED Elementary Energy InfoBook
http://www.need.org/needpdf/Elementary EnergyInfobook.pdf

NEED Energy Consumption
http://www.need.org/needpdf/infobook_activities/IntInfo/Consl.pdf

NEED Global Climate Change
http://www.need.org/needpdf/infobook_activities/SecInfo/Global.pdf

NEED History of Energy
http://www.need.org/needpdf/infobook_activities/ElemInfo/HistoryE.pdf

NEED Hydrogen
http://www.need.org/needpdf/infobook_activities/IntInfo/HydrogenI.pdf

NEED Intermediate Energy InfoBook
http://www.need.org/needpdf/Intermediate EnergyInfobook.pdf

NEED: Intro to Energy
http://www.need.org/needpdf/infobook_activities/IntInfo/IntroI.pdf

NEED: Petroleum
http://www.need.org/needpdf/infobook_activities/IntInfo/Petrol.pdf

NEED Saving Energy Student/Family Guide
http://www.need.org/needpdf/SavingEnergyStudent Guide.pdf

NEED Secondary Energy InfoBook
http://www.need.org/needpdf/Secondary EnergyInfobook.pdf

NEED Solar Energy InfoBook
http://www.need.org/needpdf/infobook_activities/IntInfo/SolarI.pdf

NEED: Wind
http://www.need.org/needpdf/infobook_activities/IntInfo/WindI.pdf

National Renewable Energy Laboratory
http://www.nrel.gov/learning/re_basics.html

Biomass Research: Learning About Renewable Energy
http://www.nrel.gov/learning/re_biomass.html

Hydrogen & Fuel Cells Research
http://www.nrel.gov/hydrogen/

National Wildlife Rehabilitators Association
http://www.nwrawildlife.org/home.asp

Natural Resources Defense Council: Renewable Energy for America
http://www.nrdc.org/energy/renewables/biomass.asp

Neoteric Hovercraft
http://www.neoterichovercraft.com/

New York Public Library On-Lion: Inventions Changed Our World
http://teacher.scholastic.com/lessonrepro/lessonplans/theme/inventions.htm

NOVA: Car of the Future
http://www.pbs.org/wgbh/nova/car/open/

PBS: Forgotten Inventors
http://www.pbs.org/wgbh/amex/telephone/sfeature/index.html

Pizza Box Oven
http://txu-solaracademy.need.org/Pizza Box Solar Oven.pdf

Power Scorecard Electricity From Biomass
http://www.powerscorecard.org/tech_detail.cfm?resource_id=1

Pure Energy Systems
http://peswiki.com/energy/Directory:Biomass

Raw Solar
http://raw-solar.com/

Renewable Energy World: Hydrogen Energy
http://www.renewableenergyworld.com/rea/tech/hydrogen

Science Learning: Ben Franklin
http://sln.fi.edu/franklin/inventor/inventor.html

SeaWorld and Busch Gardens Conservation Fund
http://www.swbg-conservationfund.org/

Smithsonian: Innovative Lives
http://invention.smithsonian.org/centerpieces/ilives/

Spotlight: Biography Inventors
http://www.smithsonianeducation.org/spotlight/inventors1.html

Squidoo: The Amazing Compressed Air Car
www.squidoo.com/compressed-air-car

Think Global Green
http://www.thinkglobalgreen.org

Think Global Green: Conservation
http://www.thinkglobalgreen.org/CONSERVATION.html

Think Global Green: Geothermal Energy
http://www.thinkglobalgreen.org/GEOTHERMAL.html

Think Global Green: Electric Vehicles
http://www.thinkglobalgreen.org/ELECTRICVEHICLES.html

Think Global Green: Natural Gas
http://www.thinkglobalgreen.org/NATURALGAS.html

Think Global Green: Nuclear Power
http://www.thinkglobalgreen.org/NUCLEAR.html

Think Global Green: Off Shore Drilling
http://www.thinkglobalgreen.org/OFFSHOREDRILLING.html

Think Global Green: Solar Power
http://www.thinkglobalgreen.org/SOLAR.html

Think Global Green: Wave Power
http://www.thinkglobalgreen.org/WAVEPOWER.html

Think Global Green: Wind Power
http://www.thinkglobalgreen.org/WINDPOWER.html

Thinkquest: Alternative Energy Resources
http://library.thinkquest.org/06aug/01335/biomass.htm

Tri-State Bird Rescue and Research Newark, DE
http://www.tristatebird.org/

United States Coast Guard: Restore the Gulf
http://www.restorethegulf.gov/

U.S. Department of Energy
http://www1.eere.energy.gov/

> **Biomass Program**
> http://www1.eere.energy.gov/biomass/

> **Energy Efficiency & Renewable Energy: Fuel Cell Technologies Program**
> http://www1.eere.energy.gov/hydrogenandfuelcells/education/

> **Energy Empowers**
> http://www.energyempowers.gov/category/Biomass.aspx

> **Hydrogen Program: Hydrogen Fuel Cells**
> http://www.hydrogen.energy.gov/pdfs/doe_fuelcellfactsheet.pdf

> **Technologies: Photovoltaics**
> http://www1.eere.energy.gov/solar/photovoltaics.html

U.S. Energy Information Administration
http://eia.doe.gov/

U.S. Energy Information Administration: Energy Kids
http://tonto.eia.doe.gov/kids/energy.cfm?page=2

> **Biofuels**
> http://www.eia.doe.gov/kids/energy.cfm?page=biofuel_home-basics

> **Biomass**
> http://www.eia.doe.gov/kids/energy.cfm?page=biomass_home-basics

> **Hydrogen**
> http://tonto.eia.doe.gov/kids/energy.cfm?page=hydrogen_home-basics

> **Wind Energy**
> http://tonto.eia.doe.gov/kids/energy.cfm?page=wind_home-basics

> **Solar**
> http://tonto.eia.doe.gov/kids/energy.cfm?page=solar_home-basics

U.S. Fish and Wildlife Service
http://www.fws.gov/home/dhoilspill

> **Effects of Oil on Wildlife and Habitat**
> http://www.fws.gov/home/dhoilspill/pdfs/DHJICFWSOilImpactsWildlifeFactSheet.pdf

Union of Concerned Scientists: Citizens and Scientists for Environmental Solutions
http://www.ucsusa.org/clean_energy/technology_and_impacts/energy_technologies/how-biomass-energy-works.html

Universal Hovercrafts
http://dev.hovercraft.com/content/

Washington State Department of Natural Resources: Forest Biomass
http://www.dnr.wa.gov/ResearchScience/Topics/OtherConservationInformation/Pages/em_biomass.aspx

World Hovercraft Organization
www.worldhovercraft.org/

Zevolution
www.zevolution.com/

Video Resources

Who Killed the Electric Car? DVD
http://www.whokilledtheelectriccar.com/

Kits

Educational Innovations: Green Science Kits Windmill Generator
http://www.teachersource.com/Energy/AlternativeEnergy/GreenScienceKits.aspx

Fuel Cell Experiement Kit
http://www.kelvin.com/Merchant2/merchant.mv?Screen=PROD&Product_Code=283698

Horizon Fuel Cell Technology Kits
http://www.horizonfuelcell.com/

Educational Innovations: Multi Project Solar Kit
http://www.teachersource.com/Energy/
AlternativeEnergy/MultiProjectSolarKit.aspx

Educational Innovations: Solar Cells
http://www.teachersource.com/Ultraviolet/
SolarEnergy/SolarCells.aspx

Educational Innovations: Solar Tube
http://www.teachersource.com/AirPressure/
RocketsAndBalloons/SolarTube.aspx

Horizon Fuel Cell Technology Kits
http://www.horizonfuelcell.com/

NEED: Solar Kit
http://www.need.org/needpdf/Exploring
SolarTeacher.pdf

Northwestern Nature Shop: The Solar Car Book and Kit
http://www.northwestnatureshop.com/Toys_
and_Games/Toys_by_Brand/Solar_Car_Kits/294.
html

Science Kit: Solar Electricity Kit
http://sciencekit.com/solar-electricity-kit/p/
IG0024377/

Siliconsolar
http://www.siliconsolar.com/solarpowered-cars.
html

Solar Energy Kit Science Kit
http://sciencekit.com/solar-energy-kit/p/
IG0022499/

Solar Home: Mini Solar Robot Kit
http://www.solarhome.org/minisolarrobotkit-
supersolarracingcar.aspx

Solar Panel Kits Science Kit
http://sciencekit.com/solar-panel-kit/p/
IG0024378/

Solar Racers
www.kelvin.com/Merchant2/merchant.
mv?Screen=CTGY&Store_Code=K&Category_
Code=TRLASR

Sun Wind Solar
http://www.sunwindsolar.com/a_scripts/
n_educational_kits.php

Thames and Kosmos: Power House
http://www.thamesandkosmos.com/products/
ph/ph2.html

World's Largest Solar Bag Science Kit
http://sciencekit.com/worldand%238217%
3Bs-largest-solar-bag/p/IG0027392/

Wind Generator Kit
http://sciencekit.com/ig0019456/p/IG0019456/

Books

Gould, A. (1986) *Great Explorations in Math and Science: Hot Water and Warm Homes From Sunlight.* Berkley, CA: GEMS

Kamkwamba, W., and Mealer, B. (2009) *The Boy Who Harnessed the Wind: Creating Currents of Electricity and Hope.* New York: Harper Collins Publishers.

Rand, Gloria. (1994) *Prince William.* New York: Holt and Company.

Smith, Roland. (2003) *Sea Otter Rescue: The Aftermath of an Oil Spill.* New York: Puffin.

Verne, Jules. (1996) *Paris in the Twentieth Century.* New York: Random House.